sexual politics
and social control

sexual politics
and social control

Frances Heidensohn

Open University Press
Buckingham · Philadelphia

Open University Press
Celtic Court
22 Ballmoor
Buckingham
MK18 1XW

email: enquiries@openup.co.uk
world wide web: www.openup.co.uk

and
325 Chestnut Street
Philadelphia, PA 19106, USA

First Published 2000

A catalogue record of this book is available from the British Library

ISBN 0 335 20669 7 (pb)   0 335 20670 0 (hb)

Library of Congress Cataloging-in-Publication Data
Heidensohn, Frances.
      Sexual politics and social control / by Frances M. Heidensohn.
         p.   cm.
      Includes bibliographical references and index.
      ISBN 0–335–20669–7 (pb) — ISBN 0–335–20670–0 (hb)
      1. Feminist criminology.   2. Women—Crimes against.
   3. Violence—Sex differences.   I. Title.
   HV6030.H38   2000
   364'.082—dc21   00–027870

Typeset by Graphicraft Limited, Hong Kong
Printed in Great Britain by The Cromwell Press, Trowbridge

For Louis

contents

preface

In writing this book I have been given help and advice by many people and at different stages in its preparation. The research reported in Chapters 4 and 5 forms part of a project undertaken with Jenny Brown, the main account of which can be found in our book *Gender and Policing* (Brown and Heidensohn 2000). I am greatly in her debt for her constant support and encouragement and her enthusiasm for our shared endeavours. Nikki Batten, Jane Creaton and Marisa Silvestri joined us in carrying out the stage of the project described in Chapter 5; their help was crucial and much appreciated. Marisa Silvestri also conducted the literature search and classification for Chapter 6. Some of the ideas and material included here were first presented at conferences and seminars where comments and criticisms showed me better ways of handling them. I am grateful to the members of the Second Australasian Conference on Women and Policing, held at the University of Queensland in July 1999, where I gave an earlier version of some of Chapter 4; Tim Prenzler, Trudy Manders, Helen McDermott, Barbara Etter, Melinda Tynan and Christine Nixon were all very helpful. I explored the issues in Chapter 5 at a research seminar at Middlesex University in March 1999 and much appreciated the responses there, notably from Susanne MacGregor, Jock Young and their colleagues.

In order to research and to write academic studies, it is vital to draw on a whole range of resources; the most crucial of these is people, and colleagues and friends with whom thoughts and ideas are shared and exchanged. All of those whom I have already mentioned have played their part, and deserve acknowledgement for this. I also want to salute Nicky Rafter, Mary Eaton and Betsy Stanko, who are always stimulating and challenging as well as being among the most companionable of criminologists. At Goldsmiths, Nirmala Rao and Tim Newburn are supportive colleagues whose own exemplary standards in research provide a benchmark. During 1996 I was a visiting professor at the Department of Sociology and Social Policy at Queen's University, Belfast. My time there was especially rewarding and I am particularly grateful to John Brewer for his thoughtful and insightful comments and for the hospitality of his department. Oliver Phillips gave me exceptional help in teaching in 1996–9; it was always a pleasure and lots of fun to work with him.

Jacinta Evans of the Open University Press was an outstandingly encouraging editor. As with every book I have written or edited, I owe an especial debt to Edmund and Lucy Pereira of ABOS who not only have, once more, prepared this manuscript for publication with enormous skill and patience, but also have done so under time pressure as their holiday dates approached.

My own experiences of policy making and implementation, and the insights these have given me into the processes involved, have been in fields not always joined to criminal justice. Nevertheless, I learned invaluable lessons from many years' involvement in the National Health Service. The numbers of people whom I worked with then are too many to mention, but I should like to single out Peter Coe and to record how much I appreciated working with him.

The British Council provided me with some funding for my visit to Australia in 1999; Goldsmiths College gave me sabbatical leave in 1996–7 when the empirical study reported here was carried out.

Families always seem to feature last in such lists although they count the most and, certainly in my own case, provide the most love, understanding and amusement. My appreciation and affection go to everyone I have mentioned; I, not they, bear the responsibility for everything here.

framing, reflecting and engaging:
problems of gender, law and order in the twenty-first century

When William Beveridge envisaged a welfare system for Britain after the Second World War, he memorably described the necessity for 'an attack upon five giant evils: Want . . . Disease . . . Ignorance . . . Squalor and Idleness' (Beveridge 1942: 170). This powerful image of the major problems 'stalking the land' caught public imagination then – the report was a best-seller – and indicated the direction and concern for the subsequent developments of social policies. More than fifty years later it was used as a title for a popular history of the welfare state (Timmins 1995).

Which giants Beveridge ignored or omitted can provide the basis for innumerable debates. I have often thought that the most striking claim to be the sixth giant can be made in the name of insecurity. By this I mean crime and all its attendant ills of victimization, fear of crime and the many costs of all kinds associated with it. This is, of course, a modern interpretation of the term: for Beveridge, insecurity meant want, lack of income. Moreover, to use it in this way reflects concerns of the later twentieth century with the long term rise in recorded crime rates, as well as the considerable politicization of the issue in Britain, which began only in the mid-1960s. This situation changed dramatically into one of 'a sharply contested politics of law and order' (Downes and Morgan 1997: 88), although in 1997, in the last general election of the century, law and order featured, but not in such a contested way (Heidensohn 1998c).

A lack of a high party political profile is not the only reason Beveridge, and his contemporaries, did not view crime or criminal justice as major concerns for social policy. The history of the interaction between welfare and law and order institutions is a complex and changing one, and Britain has some distinctive traditions in this area. Police responsibilities in other countries have included aspects of welfare provision (Bayley 1985). This has also been true at times in Britain; in his evidence to the Baird Committee in 1920, Sir Leonard Dunning, HM Inspector of Constabulary for England and Wales, described a system which he had been involved with as 'Head Constable' for the City of Liverpool in the 1890s. Because of the 'enormous number of ragged, bare-footed children in the streets, begging', a police-aided clothing association was set up which *lent* (*sic*) clothing to ill-clad children at six pence per week, after extensive police inquiries (Baird Committee 1921: 11–12, §97).

In general, however, at the time of the founding of the modern welfare institutions, law and order questions were not linked to this agenda. This was not due to a lack of concern at the time, indeed 'the Second World War produced dramatic shifts in patterns of crime' (Smithies 1982: 201), but in part, as Downes and Morgan (1997) put it, crime was seen as something like the weather, which was not susceptible to external influences. The increased political priority given to crime in the late twentieth century (successive Conservative governments ensured the passing of nine Criminal Justice Acts between 1979 and 1996) is often attributed to the sustained growth of recorded crime from the 1950s to the 1990s. While this clearly played a part, other factors were critical too: these have much more to do with the ways in which rising crime, or particular forms of offending, have been analysed, interpreted and presented and linked with other features of society.

new frameworks

Twenty-first century social science can, drawing on the challenging developments of the end of the twentieth century, take a series of concepts in which to frame our discourse about crime and social control. Key typifications include risk, victimization, globalization and gender. The literature on all of these is vast (on risk see Beck 1992; on victimization see Zedner 1997; on globalization see Woodiwiss 1996; on gender see Chapter 2). My aim here is not to add to these outpourings, but rather to pick out what seem to be the most important shifts in perception which can be linked to such work and to apply them to a series of concerns. While I share reservations with other commentators about all of these ideas, I recognize two vital aspects of them: they have *already* reshaped thinking about many matters in the late twentieth century and they have the *potential* to do so in the twenty-first century. Their importance lies as resources for those who wish to bring about change; as Lash (1995) puts it, explaining the divergences between Beck and Giddens in their interpretation of 'reflexivity in modernity',

> for Giddens . . . in late modernity a growing proportion of the population has access in more or less diluted form to sociological concepts as a hermeneutic medium of reflec-tion – and potentially as an impetus for social change – on the rules and resources of social structure.
>
> (Lash 1995: 116)

That is how I have used these concepts in this book in the linked series of essays which follow in succeeding chapters. In picking up these ideas from sources outside, if adjacent to, criminology, I am part of a tradition which I explore at greater length in Chapter 6. Criminology has to be renewed every so often from external sources or outside visitors who, as Downes (cited in Rock and Holdaway 1998: 4) neatly pinpoints, treat it as a 'rendezvous subject'. One consequence of this, as Chapter 6 makes clear, is that the production of criminological knowledge, the recogni-tion of its key influences and impact are both contentious and problematic matters. As the conclusion to that chapter suggests, the most crucial factor in determining the direction of the future of criminology may be who writes the account of its past and present and which spirits they invoke as inspiration.

It will not, then, perhaps be surprising that I have chosen to write about the topics in this volume at this time of both major social changes and of considerable *reflection* on those changes and their consequences for insecurity (J. Young 1999). One obvious reason is that gendered analysis tends to be absent from these most modern and sophisticated analyses. Take, for example, *Policing the Risk Society* (Ericson and Haggerty 1997). This is a formidable and impressive monograph, based on very detailed research in Canada, in which the authors argue that the police today use the information they gather and process on risk to control harm and danger:

> Our point is that policing consists of the public police coordinating their activities with policing agents in all other institutions to provide a society-wide basis for risk management (governance) and security (guarantees against loss).
>
> (Ericson and Haggerty 1997: 3)

This is an important and challenging work and is distinguished, unlike much else that is written about risk, by its detailed empirical and historical basis. Yet at key points where gender might be expected to be one of the aspects of the analysis, it is missing. For example a whole section of *Policing the Risk Society* (Ericson and Haggerty 1997: 256–91) is devoted to risks to identities and considers the 'police role in patrolling the borders of identities' (Ericson and Haggerty 1997: 259). The authors address age, both youth and 'seniors', race and ethnicity, but they ignore gender both as a separate category and *within* the categories that they do consider. Yet the risks, and the police attention associated with gender, are extremely well known.

The lower risks of criminality associated with females as well as the higher levels of risk and consequent 'over-attention' attached to boys and young men are not addressed. Nor are the further complexities of risk and gender: that, for example, young men are about twice as likely to be the victims of violence 'in public' as are young women, but the latter form the majority of victims of attacks in private and by intimates. The study does contain instances of such episodes, but not the kind of analysis relative to such differentials in risk, and in the *perception of risk*, where women are more likely to fear violence than men and to alter their behaviour as a result.

Some contemporary contributors to this corpus do acknowledge the significance of gender, although it is often in a somewhat marginal way, a token genuflexion, rather than true respect and consideration. Jock Young (1999) does make some attempt to include gender, observing 'the feminization of demands on law and order is a key factor in the transformation of public discourse' (Young 1999: 139). However, the only feminist agency (in any sense of that word) he gives credit to in his account of the growth of 'the criminology of intolerance' is one women's committee, imitating a Canadian model (Young 1999: 136–7). He does acknowledge the impact of feminist criminology, but cites almost no one contributing recently or currently to the field.

What is missing from Young's analysis, which has otherwise lively and lucid accounts of debates about modernity and reflexivity, is any of the sense of history and political understanding with regard to gender that he brings to the rest of his subject matter. One of the key themes of this book is the way in which gender transformations have been attempted, and sometimes accomplished, in relation to law and order, how this was achieved, and what conclusions we can draw from these experiences.

In Chapter 2, I discuss the gender politics of both waves of modern feminism; although the two stages differ in important ways, they shared pivotal concerns, over 'vice' and 'violence', which meant that social control became a major issue in both eras. In institutional terms, this meant the introduction of women as police officers in the early twentieth century and the promotion of a wide range of policies and agencies in the later twentieth century. In Chapters 4 and 5 I also consider aspects of that history and some of the problems of researching it.

Chapter 3, on the other hand, is intended to fill a gap which still remains in the literature, on whether women can be as violent as men, or whether their violence is expressed in different ways – just as other sections of the book show how women mobilized their resources to produce formidable international links, so looking at women's contribution to terrorism and political action shows that there is a continuum in their reactions to social pressures, whether from autocracy or domestic disorder. It is neither accident nor coincidence that in Britain, where some women used violence to property in fighting for the vote, the campaign to employ policewomen was the hardest fought anywhere and that some of the same women featured in both (Chapters 2, 3 and 4). These examples all illustrate a central theme of this book: not only that women have different senses of insecurity and of risk, but also that *they act on these in distinctive ways*. Most notably, they have introduced a range of formal and informal innovations to handle and reduce risk. I would suggest that such initiatives are likely to increase rather than diminish in the twenty-first century for a variety of social and historical reasons, but most of all because the politics of crime have been changing along with those of gender.

The increased visibility of victims is the single most significant shift in modern criminal justice. It is a trend by no means complete, but moving only in one direction. The (re)discovery of victims of crime came about largely through the growth of victim surveys first introduced in the USA in the 1970s and later in most western nations. The data revealed in these surveys enabled a sociology of vulnerability to becoming a crime victim to be developed. They also provided powerful resources for the growing victim movements. It is clear that governments have, certainly in Britain and the USA, seized on the lifeline which victims offer to besieged politicians. This is not to underplay the real and lasting harms done to crime victims, but to note that the prevention of crime victimization has become a substitute for crime prevention.

This effect can also be seen in the altered public agenda of policing, where issues such as the abuse of children, domestic violence and sexual assaults have been scaled up in importance (Heidensohn 1992). Again these can be seen in part as changes achieved by modern feminists, although they also relate to the earlier era too. In Chapter 2, I suggest that it is important to see how such priorities are engineered and how they may be altered. Once again, the emphasis is on *action* and I am consciously striving to counter two tendencies in current thinking. First is the confusion of feminists, who aided the discovery of victims of violence and abuse, and supported survivors of both, with victims and victim status. Second is the assumption that women have agency, when they have it at all, only in the private sphere. A quotation from Anthony Giddens best illustrates my point:

> the compulsiveness of modernity was from its first origins gender-divided. The compulsiveness documented by Weber in *The Protestant Ethic* is that of a *male public domain*. In those institutional contexts where the capitalist spirit was dominant, women were effectively left with the emotional burdens which a 'striving instrumentalism' produced. Women began modes of emotional experimentation that were subsequently to have a great impact. Yet traditional modes of gender difference, and gender domination were at the same time actively reinforced by the development of newer traditions – including the emergence of an ethos of female 'domesticity'.
>
> (Giddens 1995: 95 added emphasis)

Giddens is entitled to his own reading of *fin de siècle* history (Max Weber died in 1920). In this volume I have tried to show examples which give a counter-reading. Only a few stories can be recounted, but they include both legitimate and illegal attempts to change political systems and various forms of organization for feminist ends. Even in early twentieth century Germany, as Weber, crippled by depression, was unable to write, women whose political activity was circumscribed were able to pursue common causes with their US counterparts (Chapter 4). The present-day policewomen whom we interviewed in the 1990s are the direct heirs of early twentieth century pioneers whose aspirations and reverses they can learn from. One of the most characteristic examples of reflexivity to be found in this book is that academics can now offer interpretations of their own histories to the groups described at various points in it so that their members can, in response, achieve their own aims. (This is undoubtedly a Giddens, rather than a Beck, point about the importance of expert systems for bringing about change, Lash 1995: 196.)

The idea that we live in one world, in which many of us share the common experiences of shopping at Wal-Mart, watching the same television programmes, eating the same kind of food – franchised burgers – and where electronic communication reduces time and space to nothing, is a modern commonplace. Some of the literature on crime in late (or high) modernity does relate globalization to the other themes of this book, such as gender, but not always, and not always well. Bottoms and Wiles (1992, 1995), for instance, in several very interesting papers, note the importance of changes in the gendered nature of the labour market for crime and crime control. However, as with some of the examples already cited, they do not link up what they observe about what has been called the gender quake with the other developments they observe. This is one of the issues which I have tried to pursue here. Starting in Chapter 2, I review the literature on gender and politics, noting that Britain has been seen, until the very end of the twentieth century, as lagging behind other western democracies as far as the development of state feminism is concerned. I consider whether there may be a global pattern here, which may be followed in Britain if femocrats appear and enter government, altering its agenda to produce the common lists found elsewhere.

Not addressed directly in this chapter, but clearly a matter of some substance is the question of how truly global such an agenda can ever be, since women's basic rights to live free of attacks and abuse, are not yet universally recognized. Even if recognized, they are not always enforced. Similarly, implicit in Chapter 3 are assump-tions about and critiques of women's tendency to violence when 'liberated' and how far that has become universal. Chapter 4 has the most extended treatment of globalization in the book. There it is suggested that forms of globalization long preceded late modernity and that the earliest policewomen set up transnational police organizations in order to attain their goals of entering law enforcement and controlling their own sex. Chapter 5 presents an account of the members of the successor bodies as they participated in a conference and were observed acting out their roles.

Chapter 6 is about a worldwide institution – the academy. In it, it becomes clear that it is possible to influence histories of the development of criminology, using some of the routes discussed in that chapter.

In keeping with what I have already outlined above, I have tried to demonstrate in Chapters 4 and 5 that globalization is not a new concept or technique. Here I show it being used to strengthen the case for the introduction of policewomen, among other early twentieth century causes; it was, I argue, invented and constructed by supporters of that cause in order for their aims to succeed. For the twenty-first century there are important lessons to be learnt, especially for some of the countries of the south which need support in tackling crimes such as domestic violence.

It should be clear by now that in considering all the topics in this book, I have adopted the approach which I first noted myself some years ago (Heidensohn 1994a). After comparing find-ings from research studies over nearly three decades, on various groups of women involved with the criminal justice system, I concluded that the impact of modern feminism had affected the consciousness of women. This process I described as moving from merely 'being' to a sense of 'knowing' of an awareness of their status. Other transitions had also occurred: the women whom I had studied were more likely to 'resist' their ascribed status, less willing to 'accept' it, more ready to 'voice' dissent than to keep 'silence':

Being	→	Knowing
Acceptance	→	Resistance
Silence	→	Voice

(Heidensohn 1994a: 27)

In sum, the impact of new ways of looking at themselves had been considerable and entailed the kind of loss of both innocence and ignorance which cannot be reversed.

In the pages in this volume, I am continuing the process of discovery which I had already begun. In each Chapter I have presented a body of material designed to both inform and stimulate debate and to add to awareness, especially about the history of possibilities and change in key areas. In particular, I hope to reduce a gap which still exists between women, and some disadvantaged men and the criminal justice and social control systems. It is true that policing, the judiciary, senior management of the penal system are heavily gender-biased agencies. In earlier writing I have suggested that these may sometimes be seen as fundamentally masculine professions, whose members feel threatened by even modest female presence. Hence, so it is claimed, understandable harassment and even bullying in some settings.

There is, however, nothing inevitable about any of this. The examples set out below are both reminders and challenges. Part of the challenge lies in how contemporary feminists come to terms with some of the history which they inherit. The pioneers of the first wave were often confident, moralistic, bossy, intrusive and prescriptive. Such characteristics are the antithesis of what the early stages of modern feminism valued, where instead, deliberate structurelessness, non-institutional approaches were favoured. These are real dilemmas, but they can be faced.

The millennium era saw some major crises in law enforcement, and not just in Britain. In London, the Metropolitan Police did face a major inquiry into their handling of the murder of Stephen Lawrence, published in 1999, and a mass of attendant publicity and criticism (Macpherson 1999). In the same year, the Home Office published a review of the literature on police corruption in the UK, USA and Australia (Newburn 1999), the Patten Commission recommended major changes in the Royal Ulster Contabulary (RUC), including its name, badges and membership. In Belgium in the late 1990s, a huge scandal concerning the police and child abuse and murder threatened the political system. There were many minor and some major moral panics too, over substance abuse, the delinquency of some very young children and paedophiles in the community. The contents of this book are not intended to help calm or even 'solve' these outbreaks. It is, in any case, in the nature of the social reaction to crime and insecurity that one 'scare' will be replaced by another.

Instead, what I hope to do is to show that issues can be approached in various ways and be, at the least, rethought or diverted. The concept of insecurity, less a giant than a rather scaly monster, is now invoked to link a series of policy initiatives in relation to crime and victimization which tie them into the social policy agenda. Crime audits, local partnerships, Drug Action Teams (Home Office 1999b), a plethora of joined-up policy making has been introduced which ties criminal justice in with other agencies of the welfare system. The examples offered in this book offer some support and some challenges to such an approach.

At the very least, such developments need a new kind of politics to make them work, politics which, as I suggest in Chapter 2, draws on grassroots support in order, ultimately, to gain access to, and influence upon the state. From this follows consideration of alternative strategies for bringing influence to bear. The examples which I present to demonstrate different ways of developing such strategies are only an illustrative selection, they are not intended to be a comprehensive range. Instead, I hope that readers will consider choices of their own. With so many new initiatives in the fields of crime prevention and control, so many new 'stakeholders', so much money being spent on policies themselves and on research evaluating them, the most important questions to be raised are about the politics of criminal justice policy making and of criminology itself. The focus of this book is on the gendered aspects of this, which I believe to be among the most important 'new' features of this scene.

This does not, however, mean that this debate cannot include other groups, interests or perspectives. On the contrary, it would be possible to produce comparable accounts which bring out key issues in different ways. For example, the campaigns and struggles whereby the notion of 'risk' attached to young African Caribbean males in Britain has been redefined, albeit marginally, to include the harms that they are subject to has parallels with (and differences from) the material on gender politics. Whether one pursues a politics of difference, or one which links to specific groups also raises another set of possibilities.

For anyone who wishes to comment on, or to become involved in, such politics, there are bound to be concerns about their relationship to the state and its institutions. In the 1960s, radical sociologists of deviance declared themselves to be on the side of offenders, whom they defined as 'victims' of an oppressive, capitalist state. This led, among other things, to a period of distancing between some scholars and policy makers because the former did not want to support such practices with their research. Only with the appearance of results from victim surveys and the advent of feminist perspectives did it become clear that, however damaged and disadvantaged the young males who committed most socially predatory crime were, their victims were not rich rentiers, but their own defenceless neighbours and partners. While this 'discovery' is now widely recognized, its consequences have not yet been fully thought through. There are clear signs that this, the debate about crime, criminal justice and politics, will be the key one for twenty-first century criminologists. This book is intended as a contribution to it.

sexual politics and social control

A glance at the media coverage of the political and policy agendas in Britain at the very end of the twentieth century is highly instructive. Sexuality, whether it is stories about teenage (or even, in September 1999, two sub-teen) pregnancies or prostitution, looms large. So also do what are, essentially, accounts about contested notions and territory of law and order. By far the most notable of these, of course, concerned the Lawrence case, the Macpherson Report on the Metropolitan Police handling of the murder inquiry (Macpherson 1999) and the range of fundamental issues which this raised about racism, competence and corruption in policing.

At the same time as the Prime Minister, Tony Blair, was promoting the idea of a 'new moral order' and decrying moral decay and teenage pregnancies, two feminist commentators contributed to the same debate. One, Beatrice Campbell, responded directly to Blair's 'moral crusade' (*Guardian* 7 September 1999) and insisted that

> what really is at stake [is] less the moral well-being of these girls . . . than a panic about the faculties of the feminine body . . . For two decades, moralism has been the response of British prime ministers as they face the great tumult in society about sex, power and politics.

She went on to castigate the Prime Minister and his male Cabinet colleagues for their failure to connect with the only discourse that has had anything useful to say about all this stuff – feminism . . . contemporary feminism is not a moral manifesto, it is a space in which to take sex and power seriously as a problem of politics.

Campbell does not spell out here how she envisages an appropriate articulation of gender and politics (although she had done so elsewhere in lengthier social analyses, see for example Campbell 1993).

Alongside Campbell's riposte to the 'moral panic' about sexuality and gender, the *Guardian* published an extract from Susan Faludi's *Stiffed* (1999). Faludi is also the author of *Backlash* (1991), an account of an anti-feminist reaction that she claims set in in the USA and Britain in the 1980s in response to the second wave women's movement. In her later book, she analyses what she terms 'the Betrayal of the Modern Man'; her central thesis amounts to the view that modern men have been betrayed by their fathers and that their solution lies in a new kind of men's movement which copies some, but not all, features of feminism.

Faludi's study is only one example of a relatively new concern with masculinity as gendered and problematic. I have pointed it out because it illustrates the 'moral panic' or 'moral concern' theme of this chapter and supports my contention that gender politics and the politics of gender are crucial turn-of-the-century issues. As I shall show later, there is a remarkable congruence with the politics and social movements of a century ago and thus some valuable lessons to be learned.

presenting the problem

All the contributions I have quoted on this theme so far have highlighted issues rather than articulating them. Faludi (1999), of course, presents a lengthy case, based on six years' research, and comes closest to what I am searching for, but she does not explain how her plans for a new men's movement would be carried out. She begins with long confessions from diverse American men about their life histories, including some depressing and disturbing boasts by young men about their 'scoring' sexual encounters (some of these youths had been prosecuted for sexual offences, although only one was convicted and received a custodial sentence) (Faludi 1999).

The problems that Faludi sets out at length and Campbell covers briskly can be defined as those of *sexual politics and social control*. Both writers are justified, I believe, in focusing on the topic of gender relations as a central concern of modern society and to record the shift in emphasis to some males' activities. However, they are acknowledged 'feminist' writers and thus offering only that range of perspectives on contemporary problems. In brief, the prior issue that each addresses, albeit implicitly, is this: how can gender relations be transformed? How can such personal matters as sexuality and pregnancy be treated *politically* in a decent, dignified and humane way? Campaigns to bring about changed gender relations flourished – and met resistance as well as some success – during most of the twentieth century. There are signs of some important shifts in discourse on gender and its impact on politics in time for the third millennium. A series of familiar but important questions thus have added relevance and cogence. How do we define gender issues? How do men and women influence political agendas? How can changes be achieved in the balance of sexual relationships? Should the state be involved, or the community or the family? How can state or other organizations which are, or have been, patriarchal be altered or even captured? It has been a characteristic of several branches of feminist scholarship that they have explored these questions with some intensity in the past decades; in particular, they have addressed issues around feminist participation in and influence, on modern political life. In what follows, I try and integrate some of this inspiring work to provide a framework for exploring these themes. From this we can, I believe, draw conclusions about how to achieve more inclusive politics, which acknowledge women's (and men's) gendered positions. In doing this, I shall focus on those areas of policy and behaviour which are often seen as particularly gendered: sexuality and violence. These are also areas where the role of the state is particularly contested.

My focus here is mainly on the very end of the twentieth century and the beginning of the twenty-first century in Britain for several reasons. One is that a millennial period provides a certain vantage point for looking forward and backwards and predicting futures (Heidensohn 1996b). Second, a new government came to power in 1997, the first such electoral change for eighteen years, bringing with it very high expectations of change – the party had, after all, called itself '*New* Labour' (emphasis added). Although gender issues were not specifically highlighted during the election campaign, the numbers of women Members of Parliament (MPs) increased dramatically – by 100 per cent – and coverage of their presence and possible impact was intense and speculative immediately *after* the election (H. Jones 1998). Since then, there has not been a great deal of evidence of 'gender transformations' (Walby 1997) in British politics. Nevertheless, it is to the remaking of an established quango (a quasi-autonomous non-governmental organization) for women to which I now turn to illustrate the themes of this book.

> Rather than having a whingeing mentality, we should have a clear prioritising mentality which says these are the key issues for women in the next decade. That way, I think we will get action taken.
> (Lucy Ward, citing Baroness Crawley, in 'Tugging at the P.M's. sleeve', *Guardian* 6 September 1999)

These words are quoted from the newly appointed chair of the Women's National Commission, Baroness Christine Crawley, in an interview with the *Guardian* newspaper. She describes the makeover of this thirty-year-old organization into a 'modern, dynamic body reflecting the independent voice of British women'. The Commission's report to the United Nations Committee on the Elimination of Discrimination Against Women is noted as

> 'a fearless portrait of the inequalities still facing women in the UK' focussing on five key issues: equal pay, the balance of work and welfare, violence; a new parliamentary committee on equality and more women in public and political life.

This news story neatly encapsulates a number of major issues for anyone interested in gender and politics and, indeed, for all those wishing to bring about social change through state policies. Various tactics for influencing government policy are considered in the article: first getting 'experts in relevant fields' to produce 'lean, focused reports ministers can no longer ignore' (what one might call the 'think tank' or Fabian model). Meetings with ministers are also mentioned – an elite influencing approach – as well as what appear to be references to grassroots and feminist movements and including them and their voices within the scope of the Commission.

These topics are not mere journalistic ephemera: they raise fundamental questions about contemporary politics, policy and gender. These are addressed in media discussions such as this one, but they have been the subject too of serious academic debate. In the rest of this chapter I set out the terms of that debate, relate them to specific historic and current developments and conclude with suggestions about how political pressure might be effectively used to bring about changes in gender relations in modern British society, looking particularly at areas of crime and social control.

framing the debate

Writing about the treatment of 'gender politics and social theory' Walby (1997) categorized four types of approaches:

> to ignore gender as ... not relevant ... The second is the stage of critique when the flaws and fallacies which stem from [this] are exposed ... The third stage is to add on the study of women as a special case ... The fourth is the full theoretical integration of the analysis of gender into the central questions of the discipline itself.
>
> (Walby 1997: 137)

While this goal may not yet have been achieved, some serious attempts at reaching it have been made which help us frame questions about relations between women and men as gendered subjects and politics. In selecting and synthesizing from this literature, I have not attempted a comprehensive survey; instead, I have concentrated on approaches which engage with key questions and help formulate inquiry in insightful ways. This is intended as a contribution to further debate, which will, I believe, flourish during the twenty-first century, opening it up further and not bringing about closure.

> While there is more and more literature on gender and politics, as yet there is little which usefully links the analysis of gender, politics and the state

are the introductory words to a set of readings covering these themes (Waylen 1998). This collection raises several key issues for feminist academics and practitioners. Among these are whether 'the space can exist within the state to act to change gender relations' (Waylen 1998: 8) questions about the public–private divide and also about social movements and women's widespread participation in them. In Britain, the election of a new Parliament in May 1997, in which the numbers of women MPs doubled and five women subsequently held seats in the Cabinet, raised similar queries in debates at the level of practical politics (H. Jones 1998).

Randall and Waylen (1998: 202) offer positive conclusions following their investigation of 'the extent, means and desirability of women's participation in representative and executive political institutions' of which the most striking is that 'in order for women's political participation to be effective there needs to be a *combination* of an antonomous or grassroots feminist movement with women's significant presence within state institutions' (Randall 1998: 202, original emphasis).

A further central finding stressed here is 'the importance of the "political opportunity structure" for women's political participation' (Randall 1998: 203). In an earlier article, in which she explores the 'reasons why feminist mobilisation around the issue of child daycare in Britain has been so limited and its impact so modest' (Randall 1996: 485), she also invoked 'the changing political opportunity structure' as a major explanatory factor (Randall 1996: 502).

A chapter by Sperling in the edited collection uses McAdam's (1996) definition of political opportunity structure to explore changes in gender politics in pre and post Soviet Russia (Sperling 1998: 143–65); Randall (1998: 195–8) offers a critique of this approach in her contribution, but does not develop it further.

A perspective which does seek to integrate the theory of both gender and social movements has been developed by Taylor (Taylor and Whittier 1995; Taylor 1999); although focusing particularly on women's self-help movements, Taylor proposes a general theoretical framework which explains the emergence and development of social movements, with gender then integrated at each stage of analysis (Taylor 1999: 12–13). Taylor, like many of the contributors to this growing area of scholarship, presents her analysis as applied to several case studies of individual movements. An account which, while applying Taylor's framework, is much broader and more comparative and historically detailed, is offered by Rupp (1994) who explores the ways in which three major international women's movements organized and campaigned in the early twentieth century.

Deriving her framework from several theoretical sources, Taylor uses a threefold typology to examine the emergence and development of social movements. She outlines these as

> shifting political opportunities and constraints, the forms of organization used by groups seeking to mobilize, and variations in the ways that challenging groups frame and interpret their grievances and identities.
>
> (Taylor 1999: 12)

While she applies this analysis to a single social movement (the post-partum depression self-help movement in the USA) she demonstrates its power in unlocking some of the complexities of gender in various public arenas. For instance, she shows how this movement 'emerged from networks of feminists with clear connections to the women's movement of the late 1960s and 1970s' (Taylor 1999: 21), but that this later diminished. She charts the effectiveness of the movement in confronting and changing medical practice, although she also notes the irony that 'using gender as a framework for collective action has the potential to bolster the gendered institutions against which women take aim' (Taylor 1999: 27).

Finally, one of the most interesting analyses is that proposed by Stetson and Mazur (1995) in their set of case studies chosen to illustrate questions about what they term 'state feminism'. They define this concept as meaning 'activities of government structures that are formally charged with furthering women's status and rights' (Stetson and Mazur 1995: 1–2). A particular merit of their study is that they present, as well as fourteen cases of (largely western) nation-states, a concluding typology of women's policy machinery. This typology

> classifies women's machinery . . . according to two criteria:
>
> 1 Policy influence that is the participation of each women's policy office in the formation of feminist policies that promote the status of women and/or undermine patterns of gender hierarchy

2 Policy access, that is the degree to which women's policy machineries develop opportunities for society-based actors – feminist and women's advocacy organizations – to exert influence on feminist policies.

(Mazur and Stetson 1995: 274)

They then produce a fourfold taxonomy (see Mazur and Stetson 1995: 275, Figure 16.1). Britain, using the Equal Opportunities Commission as the sole example in the case study (Lovenduski 1995), is classified as a 'High Influence Low Access' example (Mazur and Stetson 1995: 277). From this they suggest a series of propositions about the necessary and sufficient conditions for women's policy agencies to 'reach high levels of state feminism'. These are likely to obtain when

the state is defined as a site of social justice and has the structural capacity to institutionalize new demands for equality and when society sustains widely supported feminist organizations that challenge sex hierarchies through both radical politics from outside and reform politics in unions and parties.

(Mazur and Stetson 1995: 290)

Randall comments that the term 'state femininism' can have other meanings than the one adopted by Stetson and Mazur: 'the tendency for feminists to achieve positions of influence within government' (Randall 1998: 202) being one. This distinction is important, she argues, since under what may be termed 'state-sponsored feminism' (as in the former Soviet Union and in China) there may be formal women's policy bureaucracies, but their activities have been 'severely circumscribed by the over-riding priorities and perspectives of the extremely male-dominated party-state hierarchy' (Randall 1998: 202).

However, Stetson and Mazur recognize this distinction, separating out Poland (their single East European, former communist example) as an exception in their typology of American and European states.

The importance of *Comparative State Feminism* for the framework which I am trying to construct here is that it does offer hypotheses about optimal conditions for increasing feminist influence in politics at governmental level, as well as about conditions where such influences will be lessened or fail.

In her cogent arguments about *Gender Transformations,* Walby (1997) presents us with something of a paradox in our search for guidance on enhancing gender politics. On the one hand, she insists on the reality of 'fundamental transformations of gender relations in the contemporary Western World' (Walby 1997: 1), and she gives full and detailed support for these changes and especially their impact on labour markets in Chapters 2–6 of her book. She then turns to gender politics and makes a strong case for defining 'gender politics . . . as those forms of political practice which seek to change gender relations for or against women's interests' (Walby 1997: 146).

In other words, the actions of *men* as gendered actors, especially where they oppose women's demands, need to be considered too, not least because this will show 'the full range of political forces which affect how these female actors behaved' (Walby 1997: 146). Her discussion continues with a reclamation of first wave feminism from misrepresentation, insisting that 'the breadth and radical nature of first-wave feminism are neglected' (Walby 1997: 149). She instances (and we shall return to this later) 'the campaigns around the containment of men's sexuality' as an example of both radicalism and of success and concludes that 'first-wave feminism . . . was a cross-class, multifaceted powerful political movement' (Walby 1997: 152).

Apart from statements such as these which certainly *imply* some terms for success she does not explain *how* first wave feminism achieved its goals. Instead, she turns to the topic of the 'backlash' to feminism and considers, rather than how and why it flourished, 'why did first-wave feminism end?' (Walby 1997: 159). In answer to this, she outlines various approaches: that it reached a successful conclusion, that there was organizational failure, or because of a backlash. An alternative is that 'first-wave feminism did not end in 1918, or even 1928, but has been a continuing force' (Walby 1997: 159–61).

From these approaches, some answers about the success of feminist movements might be read off: that strong, united organizational forms are critical for instance. Walby does not, however, offer any direct conclusions about optimal conditions for the rise and continuance of feminist politics. Perhaps for our discussion here, her most important contribution is the point she makes about the complexity of gender politics.

Gender politics are more complex than a simple division between varieties of feminist and anti-feminist political forces because there is a very important third position – that of the pro-women non-feminists who wish to defend and develop women's sphere of activity.

(Walby 1997: 154)

gender, governance and government

Drawing all these sources together, I suggest that Taylor's (1999) threefold framework is most helpful in setting out the social and political conditions favourable to changes in gender politics; we need, however, certainly when looking at Britain to include the dimension of the state and here Stetson and Mazur's (1995) typology, while specifically intended to illuminate the position of women's policy agencies, has wider potential. To demonstrate this and test our approach I shall apply it to two phases of significant political and development in British history: the turn of the 'old' centuries, nineteenth century to twentieth century, and of the 'new' twentieth century and twenty-first century. This is meant to be a schematic application intended to further contemporary and future debates and to provide possible answers to some of the questions outlined above. I concentrate especially on aspects of social problems called in their respective eras 'vice' and 'violence'. This is not meant to be a definitive analysis and challenges and critiques are encouraged.

'Vice' became a Victorian obsession. Social commentators deplored prostitution, especially its public visibility, but also the threat of sexually transmitted diseases to the nation's health (Walkowitz 1980; Zedner 1991). Although recent work, following the path of Foucault, 'has demonstrated that labels such as *prostitute* cannot be regarded as either valid or historical categories . . . the prostitute occupied a symbolic place' (Mahood 1990: 50, original emphasis). Nevertheless, this particular obsession of the governing classes provided middle-class (and some working-class) nineteenth century women with the experiences which led them into political activity.

Female participation in nineteenth century philanthropy is a noted and much discussed phenomenon (Prochaska 1980). Many

writers point out the opportunities which this offered to women to enter public arenas, to become professionals at their tasks
and, eventually, to engage with the political system (Banks 1981;
Rendall 1985). One of the best illustrations of this pathway into
politics is the well known history of the campaigns against the
Contagious Diseases Acts (CDA). These Acts (passed in 1864,
1866 and 1869) were designed to ensure that serving soldiers
could be protected from the consequences of using the services
of prostitutes. In garrison towns where the military were quartered,
prostitute women could be arrested, subjected to medical examina-
tion, and if found to be suffering from venereal disease, forcibly
detained and treated until they were cured. No equivalent sanc-
tions were directed at the men themselves (Petrie 1971). A Ladies'
National Association for the Repeal of the Contagious Diseases
Acts was formed in 1869 (a male organization also worked alongside it). Josephine Butler led the association through its vigorous
campaigns and eventual success (the Acts were suspended in
1883 and repealed in 1886). There were many controversies *within*
the abolitionist groups, as well as between them and those who
favoured regulation; Bland (1992: 51), for instance, describes the
real and lasting differences at the end of the nineteenth century
between 'repressive purity feminists' and their more libertarian
colleagues among the repealers.

There is very widespread agreement among historians and other
scholars over one key matter: the experiences of the campaigns for
repeal of the Contagious Diseases Acts, as well as of the widening
sphere into which these took them, led Butler and many of her
fellow campaigners into direct engagement with politics. 'Mrs
Butler and her co-workers showed themselves willing to accept
parliamentary action' (Bolt 1993: 131–2).

Although many of the moral reformers remained unsure about
parliamentary regulation of 'immorality', they were united in their
conversion into support for women's suffrage and the necessity
for a female voice in politics. There are, of course, many other
reasons advanced by historians for 'votes for women' becoming
a focus for feminists. Hollis (1987) for example has argued that
women who were, by the mid-1880s, serving as Poor Law Guard-
ians or on local school boards, sought *local* enfranchisement via
the Local Government Act 1888. She sees this as a direct claim
for political citizenship as well as a wish to extend their remit
over other areas of welfare. However, Bland (1992: 45) associates

these objectives too with furthering 'issues of morality or social purity'; she points out the multiple membership and network links between women active in these fields.

Indeed, as well as the political and social openings which the CDA and other campaigns offered, late nineteenth century women gained enormous political experience of organizing, managing campaigns and political lobbying. Harrison (1974: 319) investigated the complex interlocking membership of late nineteenth century moral reform societies (he illustrates this with a diagram which somewhat resembles the wiring of a first generation computer). Many women also acquired and tested skills of leadership and strategy that were to be deployed in the long struggle for the vote which was pursued up until the outbreak of the First World War in 1914. (There is a vast literature on gaining the suffrage; see for instance Strachey 1978; Bolt 1993.)

The vote was won relatively late in Britain (while white Australian women had gained it already in 1902) and much controversy surrounds the 'causes' of winning it and of the delays and postponements that impeded its achievement. What is most interesting to note here is how the process of emancipation and of political engagement for first wave feminist women was so closely linked to moral reform and purity movements.

It is clear that it was through claiming and occupying this ground that these women achieved the last sector of Taylor's (1999) typology *the politicization of everyday life*. Bolt (1993) summarizes this succinctly:

> Through social purity activities they were able to raise formerly taboo subjects like male and female sexuality and woman's right to control her body; could challenge the efforts of the medical profession on sexual matters, and help to transform an ancient pre-occupation with prostitution into a broad crusade to purify society.
>
> (Bolt 1993: 229)

Political debate was thus enjoined about what had once been purely private and domestic matters. Such gains in the realms of gender and politics were, of course, made at some cost. Women still focused their activities on their separate sphere: on welfare and social reform and, more controversially, on members of their own sex who were the objects of the various 'control waves' which emancipated women led. Middle-class women, by concentrating their efforts on the social regulation of the poor and disorderly, effectively *disadvantaged* working-class women, whose lives might become subject to more surveillance and control, their children and their own habits the subjects of tutelary regulation (Summers 1979; Lewis 1991; see also Chapter 5).

Some gendering of politics and some real gains in relationships between women and the state had thus been made in the early part of the twentieth century. Indeed, Walby (1997) attributes the achievement of most advances in areas such as education and employment directly to female political participation, arguing that, while there was powerful male resistance to these, gaining the franchise proved a real barrier to regression. But there were setbacks, and frustrations too. As I noted above, many comment-ators noted the class divisions in first wave gender politics; ethnic divisions were at least implicit too (Mooney 1998) even though they were sometimes addressed and overcome (Rupp 1994). The puritanical aspect of the 'social control' agenda favoured by many of these political pioneers is said to have proved an impediment to later political progress (Pugh 1992) or to have generated a particularly sexist reaction from civil servants, politicians and other members of the political establishment (Levine 1994; Doan 1997).

Relatively less attention has been given to the disenchantment that some feminists in turn came to have with political processes and their capacity to provide channels for change and improve-ment. Analyses of the origins of second wave feminism often begin with the experiences of women in the 1960s who became disillusioned with protest movements of the time, such as the New Left, anti-Vietnam War groups or, in the USA and Northern Ireland, civil rights organizations in which they were exploited and even abused by their male comrades (Rowbotham 1992: ch. 24). This history certainly helps to explain in part the initial hostility in the early years of modern British feminism either to construct conventional organizations to further its aims, or to engage in traditional party politics. As Randall suggests, the roots of this antagonism also lie deeper: 'feminists expected too much from woman suffrage . . . and . . . feminism could become so re-spectable or instrumental as to lose its radical apprehension of future possibilities' (Randall 1982: 144).

Hence the seductive, but ultimately undermining, influence of 'the tyranny of structurelessness' (Randall 1982: 164). In later work,

Randall (1987) herself and other political scientists (Lovenduski and Randall 1993) have charted a fundamental shift in the attitudes and actions of feminists in Britain, especially since the 1980s:

women's movement activists were becoming much more inclined to deal with state organizations and to attempt to work with and in established political institutions.

(Lovenduski 1995: 125)

Lovenduski is writing here about the Equal Opportunities Commission (EOC) and how, after 'the early work of the EOC proved disappointing' (Lovenduski 1995: 121), it became part of seismic change in

the 1980s . . . characterized by a sustained feminist presence in political parties, trade unions, and professional associations as well as growing feminism among members of traditional women's organizations, party sections, and women's caucuses of all kinds.

(Lovenduski 1995: 125)

Clearly, the arrival of the largest number of women ever elected to the UK Parliament in 1997 can be seen as testimony to this development. It was, of course, a planned one as far as New Labour was concerned, even though its strategy of 'women only lists' in some constituencies was prevented by successful legal challenge.

It is very clear that a vast range of late twentieth century developments offered, in the terms of the Taylor (1999) framework, huge political and social opportunities to women. Younger women especially, as Walby (1997) points out, benefited directly from the expansion of educational and economic opportunities (older women and women from some minority groups did not do so). Emphasis on formal, merit-based appointments in public life and on gender balance led to more possibilities of engaging in policy making and implementation at all levels and direct participation in politics.

In this later phase, sometimes described as 'post-feminist', organization and structure have replaced earlier 'structurelessness', not least because so many more women work within formal structures and form the majority of employees in the new service industries. The striking feature of organization, protest and campaigns in British second wave feminism is its focus on gender and violence. A late twentieth century account claims that 'during the 1980s and 1990s there has been a sea change in the recognition of male violence against women and children' (Gregory and Lees 1999: 1). The authors go on to outline the direct links from the 1970s when British 'feminists began a long-running campaign' (Gregory and Lees 1999: 1) through to major developments in the public and private sectors, policing politics and the international arena.

Rebecca and Russell Dobash have mapped these developments since their earliest days and, while their attention is often directed towards the substantive issue of domestic violence, they are always sensitive to the *politicizing* impact it has had.

> The accomplishments of the Battered Women's movements ... involved numerous crucial struggles over the recognition of the problem, recognition and legitimation of grass-roots activists, definitions of causes and solutions and construction of pragmatic and direct ways of working within these movements as well as with outside agencies.
>
> (Dobash and Dobash 1987: 169; see also Dobash and Dobash 1992)

I am not here arguing that all these campaigns have successfully accomplished their aims. As Gregory and Lees (1999) stress, much still remains to be done, and they look abroad for encouraging examples of policy innovation. Paul Rock (1988b), in contrasting his findings on the impact of victim movements and policies in Canada and Britain, noted that feminism had had markedly more influence in the former than the latter. A later study, however, which also involved extensive interviewing of key participants, came to a different conclusion.

> One of the most crucial challenges that was undertaken by the women's movement was that to traditional models of the boundaries of the 'public' and the 'private' ... such campaigns have been successful ... in relocating certain forms of violence and aggression within the public sphere ... with consequent increasing pressure on the police to recognise the pervasiveness of male violence and intervene in ways which ensure women's and children's safety.
>
> (T. Jones *et al.* 1994: 154)

However, it is more in the *interaction* within and between women and the political arena that we are concerned here. There is widespread agreement that the focus on violence has been vital for the Women's Movement and the site of its politicization (Hirschmann 1997; Stanko 1998). Lovenduski and Randall (1993) found that, in their interviews with women's officers in local government, they were particularly concerned about 'male violence against women'.

It is not hard to see the parallels between 'vice' in relation to first wave feminism and 'violence' in the history of the second wave. For both phases of the movement, a social problem which affected women's lives was brought into the public arena and became the subject of gender politics, indeed played a part in shaping those politics. There are, however, major differences. Victorian feminists moved from philanthropic work into the public sphere and political engagement because they confronted the 'double standard' in sexual morality. They sought the vote in order to have a voice in Parliament where such blatantly oppressive legislation as the Contagious Diseases Acts had been passed. Their modern successors, on the contrary, sought first to move away from the site of formal political activity to more personal campaigns. It can be said that they 'rediscovered' domestic violence which was not then on any other agenda of politicians or policy makers (Lupton and Gillespie 1994). After the successful 'politicization of everyday life' which bringing this secret and controversial issue into public debate involved, there were then movements towards political participation once again.

It is very striking that both the first and second waves of modern feminism should have been so closely linked with campaigns focused on social control. At one level, of course, there are huge differences between the issues and how they relate to the phases of feminism. Much of the crusade in the nineteenth century was about the *removal* or rejection of state regulation of women, with private and welfare-oriented solutions offered as alternatives. Twentieth century activists working in the area of domestic violence have sought, on the other hand, to move this issue out of the private and into the public sphere so that it can be acknowledged and tackled. Most significantly, perhaps, the spotlight for the early feminist moral reformers fell on women themselves, their clients did not feature very much as an issue. (It is true, of course, that Christabel Pankhurst and her mother

Emmeline did promote a movement for chastity for men at the time of the First World War.) By the time modern feminism was flourishing again, it was to the behaviour of *men*, as abusers and perpetrators of violence, that attention was directed.

Different though both periods and issues are, there are important and instructive parallels. In each era, cooperation with the state and its agencies became a central concern and generated debate about how that was to be achieved. Many themes from this debate still resonate, as I have tried to suggest in this chapter. Among the unresolved topics are those with which I began and have tried to explore. While I hope to have extended the discussion, there remains profound questions about why nineteenth and twentieth century feminists concentrated so much effort on areas of social control and whether this will be the most fruitful arena for the campaigns of the twenty-first century. It is at least now possible to consider what the prime setting for new gender politics might be and how to create it.

In outlining conditions favourable to flourishing state feminism, Mazur and Stetson (1995: 290) pinpoint 'when the state is defined as a site of social justice', when the society itself can support powerful feminist organizations. They suggest that when such conditions obtain,

> politicians and policy makers . . . are likely to set up struc-
> tures that introduce gender equity principles to many policy
> sectors and bring representatives of women's interests into
> the State to participate in that policy.
> (Mazur and Stetson 1995: 290)

It can be argued that those conditions obtain, *or* that pressure can be brought to ensure that they do. There is a case for arguing for 'rejectionism', that women, and disadvantaged men, should not engage with formal state apparatus which cannot be adapted to serve their needs and may incorporate or corrupt them. But it is possible to argue the opposite view, that engaging in political endeavour can bring about some benefits for women, and, indeed, that rejection or abstention can change nothing. I have tried to show that, in terms of the model, the time could be right for further political involvement and the development of more gendered politics. The structures and the issues are in place. Is there anything to lose?

three

sex and violence

This is an account by an eye-witness of an attack on a police officer which was nearly fatal:

> William Henry Jones told how he '. . . saw the whole of them strike the officer Chapman, and if they had not been prevented [they] would have killed the officer. The girls were the chief cause of the disturbance.'

When Police Constable Chapman recovered and gave evidence in court he and other witnesses testified to the brutality of the beating he received from the women in the gang (A. Davies 1999: 84–5). This incident, which took place in Salford, is not an example of the kind of episode which has been highlighted by the late twentieth century media to demonstrate that females have now become 'deadlier than the male' (Kirsta 1994). In fact, it happened in June 1890 and is one of a number of examples cited by Andrew Davies to support his view that young women were active in gang fights in the Manchester area in the late nineteenth century and, more frequently, in 'collective assaults upon local people and the police' (Davies 1999: 72).

I have quoted this historical case study because it provides a telling departure point for examining another of the key issues in the gender, law and order complex. Violent crime continued to be a major public concern at the end of the twentieth century and its reduction a focus for official policies. A federal law, passed in the USA in 1996, required the Attorney-General to review a report on the effectiveness of crime prevention programmes 'with special emphasis on factors that relate to juvenile crime and the effect of these programmes on youth violence' (quoted in Sherman *et al.* 1998: 2). All the major political parties in Britain stressed the need to create secure communities in their 1997 election mani- festoes, emphasizing fear of crime as well as actual offending as harmful (Heidensohn 1998c).

There have been significant shifts in the appreciation of gender factors in violent behaviour. Most notable of these has been the highlighting of domestic violence, especially the battering of women by their partners (see for example Office for Victims of Crime 1998; Hanmer *et al.* 1999). A further development, however, is the trend to analyse and present males as both perpetrators *and victims* of crime. In their extensive analysis of lethal violence in North America, Zimring and Hawkins (1997) emphasize the gendered and the racialized concentration of homicide in the USA:

> the likelihood that African Americans will be involved in homicide either as victims or offenders is far greater than their proportionate share of crime . . . the more life-threatening the offence, the greater the concentration of both victims and offenders among African Americans.
> (Zimring and Hawkins 1997: 87)

The majority of both groups will be male. In a similar way, the male contribution to both violence and victimization has been addressed in Britain and other countries in the 1990s (Newburn and Stanko 1994; Jefferson 1996).

Indeed the one issue which received relatively less attention in research is that of female violent offending. At the same time, there has been media concentration on a number of high profile cases involving women perpetrators, as well as serious journalistic reports which draw on these and, to some extent, reflect their somewhat sensational tones (MacDonald 1991; Kirsta 1994; Lloyd 1995). A body of research has been produced which can be used to illuminate some of the questions which discussing women's violence gives rise to. It is clear that most modern feminist re- search has focused on women as victims (see Heidensohn with Silvestri 1996; see also Chapter 6). Apart from the values and interests which inform such choices of research topics, it is also still the case, as I shall outline later, that women account for a smaller share of recorded crime than men and that their contributions to violent offending are modest, thus centring the focus of inquiry on their lower performance, rather than as a major social problem.

There are, despite low rates of recorded violence by women, areas of concern; moreover, in the twenty-first century these still bear a disconcerting resemblance to those of the pioneer days of feminist perspectives in criminology. Debates about female exceptionalism, and hence their chivalrous *or* more severe treatment by the courts, recur (Lloyd 1995) as do minor moral panics about female 'carer' killers (N. Davies 1993) or girls in gangs. These debates are not artificial, although the issues are often sensationalized or trivialized by the mass media (Naylor 1998). They can have important consequences for women offenders themselves (Heidensohn 1995) and their families; they may be linked to wider issues such as the participation of women in the armed forces, especially front-line combat, and in law enforcement, even to taking part in contact sports such as boxing and wrestling. Significantly too, variations on the 'liberation causes crime' argument (see below) are introduced to imply that females who seek equality are likely to pay for this in increased rates of victimization, because they are a threat to masculinity (Tomsen 1997: 100).

In the rest of this chapter I want first to put all these themes in historic and social context, then to look at what has happened to trends in female recorded violence, linking these observations with the theorizing and research on the topic, before suggesting how these subjects might be considered in fresh ways in the twenty-first century. First of all, a brief note on the interpretations of the term 'violence' which I have adopted. Following the *Oxford English Dictionary* (*OED*), I have largely used the meaning given there: 'the exercise of physical force so as to cause injury or damage to a person, property, etc.'. This definition itself raises the matter of force and I have extended my approach to include situations where force is used which may well be legitimate, because violence, sanctioned or not, can occur. (It is an ironic coincidence that the first illustrative quotation in the 1993 edition of the New Shorter OED is from Pat Barker: 'Men fought ... but violence between women was unthinkable'.

There can be no doubt about women's violent potential. Women were significant contributors to violent revolutionary movements in the past two centuries. Charlotte Corday infamously assassinated Jean Paul Marat; more notably women radicals played important parts in organized violence and terror in later struggles. The *pétroleuses* of the Paris Commune have probably been misrepresented (Thomas 1967) but it is clear that women were considerably involved in that conflict. Women were key figures in the early years of the Russian Revolution and were in the plots to murder Tsar Alexander IX, including the final successful one in 1881 (Broido 1977). The first British feminist movement split over the issue of legal tactics, with the suffragettes of the Women's Social and Political Union using means such as breaking windows, damaging paintings and a campaign of arson, while the suffragists rejected them, in order to achieve the vote.

Female terrorists have been participants in all the modern campaigns of political action, although their participation *rate* varies considerably (MacDonald 1991). The Red Army Faction (the Baader-Meinhof Group) in Germany had a woman leader and women formed about half its known members (Becker 1977). Women played a prominent part in the early stages of the Irish Republican Army (IRA) campaigns in Ireland, but their role was diminished later. Other political protest movements continued to encourage women participants, sometimes as suicide bombers in India and Sri Lanka, for instance. One manifestation of female protest action in the late 1990s was to be found in animal rights and other 'eco-terrorism' in which women played a significant role (Critcher 1996).

Political violence may seem exotic and unusual and is, of course, remarkably rare. At least two other phenomena confirm my initial assertion. Modern warfare has increasingly involved women: the Gulf War highlighted the deployment of women as front-line troops. There is much debate about whether they should be there at all (Enloe 1988, 1993). Opposition to their military role comes from feminists who see all warlike involvement as oppressive and from conservatives to whom it is unfeminine. Pragmatists fear the effect on male soldiers, distracted by either sex or chivalry when in battle. Nevertheless, they were there in the US forces in the Gulf, later in the Balkans and had already been engaged in battle in the invasion of Panama. Women also play a role in the armed forces (though less usually in direct combat) of most North

Atlantic Treaty Organization (NATO) countries and in those of many others, including Israel and Syria. British forces were also integrated during the 1990s, with women increasingly taking senior positions, although several highly publicized cases of alleged harassment and other media stories caused embarassment.

Women's access to the legitimate use of arms and of physical force has also been notable in the police and security forces of many nations. Female officers joined the police in the USA, Britain and several European countries early in the twentieth century (Martin 1981; Carrier 1988; Heidensohn 1992). Their work was mostly confined to child protection and the welfare of women and girls. In the 1970s women's roles in most police forces changed with special women's bureaux and units being abolished and women officers being absorbed into all types of police work, including crowd control, marksmanship and so on. These developments have also been contested (S. Jones 1986). Neither the armed forces nor the police have become feminized. They do, however, recruit steady, if modest, numbers of female recruits and arm and train them to use deadly force (Brown and Heidensohn 2000).

None of this may be as novel as it seemed in the 1990s. Myths of Amazons and other female warriors have abounded for centuries. While there does not appear to be strong evidence for the existence of groups of Amazons in the past – bands of female warriors who fought fiercely together – there are a number of established cases of women who enlisted in armed services and fought in past conflicts, disguised as men. Joan of Arc is perhaps the best known and attested case. Whether or not such stories are true is irrelevant; the point is that they have been believed at various times and it is certainly demonstrable today that women can be licensed by the state to kill.

Stark's (1996) researches into British naval warfare led her to conclude that

> these are verified accounts of more than twenty women who joined the Royal Navy or Marines dressed as men in the period from the late seventeenth century to the early nineteenth century.
>
> (Stark 1996: 82)

She observes that, since these were cases where the true identity was revealed, there must have been 'others whose male disguise was never penetrated, and whose stories have therefore gone unrecorded' (Stark 1996: 82).

Of women who are known to have joined the British army, the most famous was Dr James Miranda Barry, who qualified as a doctor and then served for forty-six years as a physician and surgeon, becoming Inspector-General of the Medical Department and was found after her death to be female (Garber 1992: 203). Barry, of course, did not have a combat role in the army, but another woman who wrote her own story did, serving as a cavalry officer in the Russian Army during the Napoleonic Wars. Nadezdha Durova (1989) wrote a popular memoir of her time in the military, received a pension and was buried with full military honours, having fought in numerous engagements and won medals.

In the history of violence there seems to be little that women have not been prepared to do, or to assist in. Most violence occurs, of course, in private, especially domestic settings. Women have beaten or attacked or slain their close relatives (H. Allen 1986). Some of these cases have become notorious: Lizzie Borden of Fall River, who probably murdered her parents with an axe (she was acquitted), had plays, poems, songs and books written about her. Still more notoriety has attached to women whose violence has been 'public', directed at strangers. Myra Hindley's case still provoked outrage over thirty years after her trial for the Moors murders. The much publicized case of Carole Wurnos concerned an alleged female serial killer in Florida, who shot and killed men who gave her lifts (*Guardian* 7 February 1991).

Later in the 1990s other notable cases of female serial killers attracted worldwide attention. In 1993 Beverley Allitt was convicted of four murders of children in her care, of attempting to murder three who survived her attacks and of inflicting grievous bodily harm on six other children (N. Davies 1993). Rosemary West was convicted of the murders of ten young women, many of whose bodies were found buried at her family home in Gloucester. At the end of the 1990s, a series of trials of women accused of the murder or manslaughter of children in their care in both the USA and Britain received extensive media coverage.

I do not intend to repeat a litany of horrible offences: there is a rather repellent genre of such accounts which juxtapose evil and depravity with the feminity of the prepetrators. All these examples show, I believe, that women do not lack the capacities to be violent to others, nor indeed to themselves.

trends in female violence

There is still a considerable gender gap in criminality, whether recorded arrest and conviction rates or self-report studies are used as the measure, even though some convergence has occurred. Self-report studies show fewer young women than men ever admitting committing an offence: 31 per cent of females but 55 per cent of males aged 14–24 reported ever offending. In 1997 only 17 per cent of the known offenders dealt with by the British criminal justice system were female. In general women are likely to have shorter careers in crime, are less liable to be convicted for repeat offences and their most common indictable offences (accounting for 59 per cent of female offenders in 1997) are theft and handling stolen goods (all figures are taken from Home Office 1999a).

Numbers of women convicted or cautioned for offences of violence against the person rose during the 1990s, although they levelled off at the end of the period, but the numbers of men declined somewhat during the same decade. Women's share of violent offending remained low and violence still constituted a minor share of female criminality at 10 per cent or less (Home Office 1999a). In the USA more consistent, and more noticeable, upward trends have been logged over a twenty year period. In 1975 women were 13 per cent of all arrestees, but 19 per cent in 1995; women constituted 10 per cent of the arrests for violent crime in 1975, but this had risen to 14 per cent in 1995 (National Criminal Justice Reference Seminar (NCJRS) 1998). Although women are, as in Britain, still relatively modest contributors to crime rates, increased arrest rates for juvenile females were a feature of these two decades. The rate for girls went up by over 100 per cent for violent crime between 1981 and 1995 (Poe-Yamagata 1996), over 160 per cent for aggravated assault and by nearly 200 per cent for weapons offences. For all these offences, arrest rates for boys grew at a much slower rate, often by only half the rate of increase, while, of course, the *numbers* involved were far greater. It is such relatively larger rates of increase which have attracted attention and concern as well as the sensational reporting of a few cases (Kirsta 1995). Prominent health warnings must be attached to such figures.

Sources other than official crime figures can be used to study trends, although even more wariness is appropriate. The National

Society for the Prevention of Cruelty to Children (NSPCC) pub-
lishes reports, based on its registers of abused and at risk children.
Between 1983 and 1987 some 8274 children were placed on
these registers. Of these 77 per cent had been abused and 23 per
cent were thought to be at risk of abuse (Creighton and Noyes
1989). The NSPCC report provides very detailed analysis of the
suspected perpetrators of abuse, including data on their relationship to the children. In the period covered by this study, natural
mothers were implicated in 33 per cent and natural fathers in
29 per cent of the physical injury cases. However, when the figures
are adjusted for whom the child was living with, then the natural
fathers were implicated in 61 per cent and mothers in 36 per cent.
In 1989, some 3589 children, a considerable (34 per cent) increase
on 1988, were registered. The suspected perpetrators' share of
physical abuse did not alter much, with figures of 61 per cent
and 33 per cent respectively (NSPCC 1990). NSPCC registers cover
some 10 per cent of the children living in England and Wales.
These figures are not, of course, for convictions or cautions. It is,
thus, perhaps even more remarkable that mothers, and other
female carers, were not implicated more often, especially since
these findings do not indicate the *length* of time spent with the
child. It seems highly likely that mothers, stepmothers and others
were more often alone and for longer periods with the child. Yet
children appear to be more at risk from males at home than
females. Fairy tales and Christmas pantomines ritually celebrate
the stereotype of the wicked stepmother, but it is stepfathers
who are more of a possible menace.

   I have pointed out the dangers of using material of this kind
to suggest women's 'real' violence. There are, nevertheless, some
points to be made in favour of doing so, if only in relation to
this area. True, scepticism about police-based crime figures has
probably never been greater (see M. Young (1991) for an account
of their manufacture and massage to improve clear-up rates). Yet
this scepticism has led to a series of alternatives being produced
with which official sources can be 'triangulated' (Jupp 1989). As
I have indicated, all the available time series show a significant,
if varied, gender ratio. This may well be a social construct, but
if it is its production needs to be explained. Such reports are
all produced for policy purposes and thus reflect acts committed
in the name of agencies and also form the basis of future
decisions.

Other sources, chiefly of a local and qualitative kind, do exist. Broadly speaking, such studies confirm two points already observed: first, there is a notable gender ratio in violence in favour of women, and second, while women commit comparatively little violence, their violent behaviour is quite varied. In her study of street crime in Brixton, Burney (1990) found one female mugger (and fifty males). Researchers have observed girl gangs (or, more often, girls in gangs) and girls who fight (Shacklady Smith 1978; A. Campbell 1981, 1984). However, these are relatively rare sightings in a vast forest of studies which depict male gang delinquency and especially the centrality of fighting to it (Willis 1977; Corrigan 1979). One contentious topic is the amount of hidden domestic violence, most of it, it is assumed, committed by men against women (Stanko 1990).

There are a number of qualitative studies which let women's own voices express their feelings about violence and a few (a very few) which are autobiographical. Carlen (1983, 1988) in her series of unsurpassed ethnographies of women offenders has highlighted the central role violence plays in many of their lives. Most of those whom she interviewed at Cornton Vale Prison in Scotland had lived in violent relationships, often being the victims of multiple beatings.

> 'Melissa' in for attempted murder said 'you can take so much violence towards your own person, then you will retaliate . . . I'm fed up with getting battered . . . you don't care what you've got in your hand'.
>
> (Carlen 1983: 43)

In her later study of thirty-nine women's criminal careers, Carlen notes that while fourteen of them had convictions for violence against the person, only three had committed these acts for gain (Carlen 1988: 20). A significant group, who had mostly been in care when young, had belonged to 'hell-raising gangs' which had fought others for fun and excitement; 'if there's other gangs give us dirty looks, we just go and fight with them' (Carlen 1988: 19).

By the time they were a little older these women had begun to realize the costs to them of their teenage fun in stigma, loss of freedom and of wider opportunities. Violence committed by them when they were older was, Carlen asserts, always when they felt threatened. Most told her that they had been forced either to fight or threaten violence in order to survive family life, street life, care, welfare surveillance, Borstal, police station and prison.

(Carlen 1988: 22)

Carlen acknowledges a gulf between herself and her subjects over the role of violence in their lives and its meaning to them, a gulf which was not bridged: 'you wouldn't understand' (Carlen 1988: 22). Violence was 'a fact of life' for them (seven had been battered by partners, others by fathers and three had been sexually abused by their fathers).

Ethnographic studies 'on the street' in US cities have produced telling and varied descriptions of the use of violence by women. In her account of the Brooklyn drug market, Lisa Maher argues that women users present themselves in a violent or crazy way as a strategy for survival, to ward off harm or attack (Maher 1997: 95). Miller (1998), reporting a comparative study of male and female violent street robbers in St Louis, Missouri, found common motivations 'for both women and men . . . motivations to commit robbery are primarily economic . . . but they also include elements of thrill seeking' (Miller 1998: 47). Miller is somewhat sceptical of the argument that females employ violence to protect themselves (Miller 1998: 60) but she did not find equality among her street sample. Rather, her respondents described a highly gendered environment to which they adapt their activities in order to rob successfully: chiefly by robbing other women, using threats and weapons and by exploiting men's susceptibility to women. In consequence, they do carry out their crimes differently from males who are more aggressive, direct and 'masculine' (Miller 1998: 47).

Relatively few women, as we have seen, commit crimes and still fewer acquire records for serious, violent offending. The dearth of autobiographical accounts by women of their criminal careers (Heidensohn with Silvestri 1996) is not, however, solely due to this. Rather, it seems to stem from the disavowal of deviance, the resistance to stigma which women manifest more than men. While there are accounts of the use of violence for political ends by women such as Rosa Luxemburg (Nettl 1969) and Christabel Pankhurst these are not personal stories. (The suffragettes, of course, conducted an escalating campaign of arson and damage in 1912, but did not use violence against people except in a symbolic way to ensure arrest.)

There is a recognized pattern of male 'lifestyle' violence in which young men fight and brawl, often after heavy drinking and in ritualized forms (Tomsen 1997). As Jock Young (1988) has pointed out such fighting has a certain moral symmetry: victims and perpetrators resemble each other and may be doing as much harm as they receive. Women, however, are different. Their assailants are mostly male and females rarely retaliate. Edwards (1989: 127) notes that 'in England and Wales . . . dramatically higher numbers of husbands kill wives than wives kill husbands'. This is in contrast to the USA where, as in so many matters, there is greater equality.

Research on female homicide patterns in Australia comes to similar conclusions and also that 'women rarely killed out of jealousy or depression (the dominant themes for males) and instead most were responding to precipitating violence from their partner' (Polk 1993: 161).

In another Australian study of women who killed their children, Alder and Baker (1997) note the diversity of the scenarios among their cases and also challenge the notions of 'loss of control' and 'emotional outburst' to explain these cases. On the contrary, they argue, 'these acts by women are undoubtedly highly emotional; at the same time, however, they do not necessarily represent a sudden loss of control' (Alder and Baker 1997: 34). However, writing about a sample of English 'filicide' cases, Wilczynski pointed out that most women offenders (64.3 per cent) 'use "psychiatric" pleas', whereas only 30 per cent of men did so (Wilczynski 1997: 422).

theories of female violence

Whereas it was once an area ignored by criminologists, the topic of women and crime was one of the most discussed in the late twentieth century literature. The main source of this change has been the development of feminist approaches to criminology. The authors of one major text call this 'the most notable development in theorizing about deviance' (Downes and Rock 1988).

Growth in this field has been rapid, rich and diverse. The ensuing harvest of scholarly produce has been usefully characterized as focusing on two key concerns (Daly and Chesney Lind 1988). These, in simple terms, are first, the remarkably robust sex crime ratio in which recorded male criminality (more or less) always exceeds female criminality – 'the gender ratio problem' – and second, whether theories of crime and deviance, invariably presented as universal, are in fact specific to males and cannot be applied to females (Heidensohn 1968; Smart 1977; Heidensohn 1996, 1997c) (the generalizability issue).

past perspectives

Three kinds of approaches to female violence can be distinguished:

- theories of an 'iceberg' of hidden female crime
- pathologies associated with female violence
- mainstream sociological theories applied to females.

Pollak (1950) is perhaps the best known exponent of the 'iceberg' thesis. He argued that women were responsible for *more* crime, especially violent crime, than men. Their position in the family enabled them, in his view, to poison and kill undetected and their physiology and psychology made dissembling easy. Pollak's work has been widely challenged (for example Heidensohn with Silvestri 1996) but was accepted as valid for a long time. Its main weaknesses are the lack of evidence and of explanations for male connivance in this situation.

Psychopathological states peculiar to women have been claimed as impelling women to violence. Infanticide is legally defined as the homicide of an infant perpetrated by a woman affected by pregnancy and lactation. In modern times premenstrual tension – or syndrome – has been highlighted as an aetiological factor in much female behaviour including violent crime and, in particular, murder (Hey 1985; Reynolds 1991). There are many problems with such theories, but from a sociological point of view there are primarily two. First, they tend grossly to overpredict rates and trends of female violence, and second, they tend to treat as inherently pathological the 'natural' female states of menstruation, parturition, lactation and menopause.

Mainstream sociological theories are frequently alleged to apply to female as well as male behaviour. Some examples of theses about juvenile gang crime have been so applied, such as subcultural and strain theories. Campbell (1984) outlined the careers of three New York girl gang members. They all acknowledge their fighting pasts. Campbell made it clear that her subjects' lives were influenced subculturally in their gender roles, which tended to be somewhat stereotyped, even traditional. While this application of subculture theory is in itself successful, there are problems with its generalizability to other groups and cultures.

'feminist perspectives'

Since the rise of feminist approaches in criminology two other perspectives have been developed:

- the liberation leads to violence thesis
- theories of the marginalization and exclusion of women, some of whom may become offenders.

The so-called 'liberation hypothesis' was first suggested by Adler (1975), who insisted that a new female criminal had appeared in the 1970s following the rise of modern feminism; this figure sought equality through toughness and violence in street crime. Adler's assertions about 'new' female violence are not well supported statistically nor can links between female violence and emancipation be substantiated. Most female violence, as we have seen, is traditional and within the family and not street or predatory crime. Nor are female offenders feminist in their views, indeed numerous research studies have suggested that they are conventional in their views of gender roles (see Naffine (1987) for a useful review).

While some North American criminologists pursued these arguments, their European counterparts have concentrated on theories of the increasing marginalization and even exclusion of women from social and economic life especially in the late twentieth century (Cain 1990; Heidensohn 1991). Such approaches have some explanatory power but are not especially directed at violence and indeed are primarily used to explain prostitution and petty property offending.

The most promising developments theoretically are those that incorporate feminist perspectives with existing sociological theories which have explanatory power. Heimer and De Coster (1999), for example, use an adapted form of diferential association theory linked to feminist theories of power differences to analyse and compare male and female youths' violence. They argue that 'the violent delinquency of females is controlled through rather subtle, indirect mechanisms, while the violence of males is controlled in more direct, overt ways' (Heimer and De Coster 1999: 277). Their analysis also shows the interaction between variables such as gender socialization and structural position so that, while social disadvantage is strongly associated with violent delinquency, so are traditional views of gender roles, and hence, boys are more likely to commit violent acts than girls (Heimer and De Coster 1999: 305). This approach returns us to the example cited at the head of this chapter: in nineteenth century Manchester and Salford, Andrew Davies (1999) observes, aggression and rioting by young women were heavily castigated by magistrates and others, but in practice they were usually sentenced more leniently and frequently handed over to their parents for private and informal chastisement. As Davies (1999) points out, contrary to many historical analyses, the young 'viragos' of this period were far more rebellious than their male counterparts since they transgressed boundaries of both gender and criminal law.

conclusions

Several commentators on this topic have pointed out that feminist scholars have avoided it (Alder and Baker 1997). This can lead to the gap in research being filled by unsubtle and unsympathetic accounts (Simpson 1991) even though such hesitancy is understandable.

> Feminist scholars have been hesitant to grapple with the issue of women's violence, both because a focus on women's violence draws attention away from the fact that violence is predominantly a male phenomenon and because studying women's violence can play into sensationalized accounts of female offenders.
>
> (Miller 1998: 60)

It is, nevertheless, important that such work should be conducted and its scope expanded. The new millennium offers women many more opportunities than ever before, at least in the prosperous nations of the north. Women now take part in many contact sports, including bouts of boxing between women and mixed male and female contests (*Observer* 10 October 1999). Women are joining armies and police forces in growing numbers too. Predictions that such forms of 'liberation' lead to outbreaks of female violence have been voiced in the past and have not materialized (Adler 1975). Yet there are important issues to address. We do not have much evidence about the impact on women of their involvement with the use of (legitimate) force, or indeed vice versa.

While women in some richer countries can face the twenty-first century taking part in 'emancipated' activities, women in the poorer South still face the threat and the reality of serious physical violence and the problems of real restrictions on their freedom (Joutsen 1999). Future research on female violence will have to take account of considerable differences within and between groups of women and their experiences. In many parts of the world, even in the twenty-first century, women are beaten and abused, sold into the sex trade and trafficked like stolen goods; often they have no rights of redress against rapists or batterers. New research needs to consider these agendas, where violence by women might be expected to be more prevalent, if only in retaliation or self-defence.

Researchers have concluded that female participation in crime *fell* in eighteenth and nineteenth century London (Feeley and Little 1991) especially in relation to more serious offences. They suggest that there has been long term decline in interpersonal violence in England, a civilizing process has taken place in which such violence has been increasingly prohibited and subject to sanction: 'these "civilizing processes" affected women first, in so far as they were viewed as the moralizing influence in society' (Feeley and Little 1991: 749). But such controls might slip or shift and, in any case, their mechanisms and operation are not well understood.

In relation to our key themes of gender, law and order, female violence remains something of a conundrum. Violence remains, mainly, 'a man's game' – but not wholly so. It has been chosen by more young women than used to be the case, but we cannot say for certain why, or how, trends will move. For many people, these will become important areas of debate and conflict. In Chapter 2, I outlined ways to strengthen gender politics. This issue surely merits serious consideration within that framework.

There are projects which will assist in achieving better understanding of this issue under way, although much still remains to
be learnt. It is also a topic which reminds us of a different way of
taking action.

global networks and women in policing

Concerns about the transnationalization of policing form a new and challenging area for social science research, part of a much wider agenda of globalization. Yet, as James Sheptycki (1995) has emphasized, such 'concerns with transnational criminality are by no means a recent phenomenon', citing the origins of the idea of Interpol in 1914 and conferences on the 'war on drugs' in 1909 and 1912 (Sheptycki 1995: 616). In a more recent article he has argued that 'policing [was] in a sense, transnational from the outset' (Sheptycki 1998: 496), basing this view on the exportation of the colonial model beyond Europe and the early formation of the International Association of Chiefs of Police. In this chapter we focus on a distinctive area of globalization in policing which is also characterized by such a paradox: the international organizational developments are comparatively recent, yet they have their roots in social changes and movements in the nineteenth and early twentieth centuries. Indeed, in some ways, those origins still influence current practice and (as we shall seek to show) provide the keys to understanding the history and trends we shall explore.

globalization and gender

The role of policewomen and its globalization is our theme here. We contend that from, or even *before*, the earliest days of women's entry into law enforcement, the pioneer policewomen sought to construct a concept of the international woman police officer, and even to develop a movement with worldwide span and support. A century later, although there have been vast changes in policing, its context and in gender relations, this is still an aim, as we shall show. We shall also present arguments as to why this happened, consider its significance and predict future trends.

The entry of women into policing and their subsequent impact have been depicted in a number of ways. Carrier (1988) sees the long and contested struggle for attested status as an equal opportunity campaign which had an ironic outcome: women policing women. Schulz (1995), writing of the USA, describes the arrival of social workers with badges, which was a costly diversion, whereas Appier (1998) claims that US policewomen had a profound effect, forcing a gender division of labour in policing and the development of the modern masculine, crime control model. Pugh (1992: 34) attributes the failure of feminism between the wars in Britain to dislike of the women patrols and their curbing of 'vice' in the First World War. For some feminist writers, there is evident discomfort in acknowledging that women sought control over their own sex and were eager to be uniformed agents of patriarchal authority. Jeffreys' (1985) claim that 'the movement to institute a women's police service was integrally connected to the campaign against the sexual abuse of children' (1985: 60) is described by Levine (1994) as 'overstated in the light of actual practice . . . the greater proportion of female work . . . continued to focus principally on the disciplining of working-class women' (Levine 1994: 51).

Other commentators have acknowledged this (Lock 1979; Heidensohn 1992) but have not always recognized how much the earliest proponents of a role for women in law enforcement were involved in an international development. Looking at these developments through the framework of transnational policing enables us to reinterpret both past and present and to suggest how the future of the contemporary alliances may proceed.

origins and destinations

The role of women, especially middle-class, Protestant women, in promoting the causes of the mid-nineteenth century is well established. They campaigned against slavery, for peace and temperance. Later they turned to moral and social causes. In Britain notably, the campaigns against the Contagious Diseases Acts (see above) gave experience to Josephine Butler and her associates, who expanded their organization and their cause purposefully as they became willing to work with and within the state framework to legislate and criminalize,

> in 1875 Mrs Butler established the first international organisation for moral reform . . . [this] gave British feminists a leadership role in transnational humanitarianism that had been occupied in the antebellum period by their American sisters (for example in anti-slavery, temperance and peace) and would be held by them again in the drive to bring about international cooperation among suffragists and temperance workers in the 1880s.
>
> (Bolt 1993: 131)

Campaigns to introduce prison and police matrons are seen by many historians as the direct forerunners – the practice runs, almost – for the introduction of women as police officers (Feinman 1994; Schulz 1995). From our viewpoint in this study, there are instructive parallels to record. First, where change was affected in the treatment of women in the criminal justice system in this period it is generally characterized by the pressures brought by women *organizing* – by recruiting support, lobbying and campaigning using existing alliances or creating new ones. The Women's Christian Temperance Union (WCTU, founded 1874) is a good example of this. Second, the part played by *voluntary* effort was crucial. The matron campaigns run by the WCTU were successful in part because they originally provided unpaid matrons or helped to subsidize the posts (Schulz 1995).

It was with women in their own community or at least in specific parts of it – in slums, on the streets, in impoverished homes – that nineteenth century women most sought to intervene with and upon their own sex. In mid-Victorian England prostitution or 'vice' had come to be seen as the greatest social evil of the day (Walkowitz 1980). The state attempted to control this 'ill' as a public health matter through a series of Contagious Diseases Acts passed in the 1860s. As a consequence, women in garrison towns who were identified as common prostitutes could be arrested, examined and, if found to be suffering from venereal disease, forced to undergo treatment in a 'lock' hospital. Working-class women were most affected by the Acts (soldiers themselves were not subject to any such regulation) but the alliance set up to campaign for the repeal of the Acts was led by Josephine Butler, a 'lady' of upper-middle-class background and included middle- and working-class women and men and groups such as trade unions (Petrie 1971). The Acts were finally repealed only in 1886, by which time the campaigners had extended their activities to Europe and to trafficking in women as well as 'moral rescue' work.

Considerable numbers of (mainly) middle- and upper-class women became involved in forms of moral and social reform work in the later nineteenth century. One contemporary estimate suggested that some half a million women were working in charitable activity (Hubbard 1893, cited in Prochaska 1980: 29). Historians point to several key aspects to this development: these women were able to take advantage of the 'feminization' of charitable work – for example the growth of social case work – to move into a public sphere where they could have a role (Mooney 1998: 85). Moreover, they had highly developed networks which both offered sources of support and provided the basis on which work was organized (Vicinus 1985; Morrell 1996). Many of the organizations which women formed at this period had overlapping membership; Harrison (1974: 319) examined members of fourteen bodies in 1884 and found them to be closely linked in moral reform, feminism, temperance, Sunday observance and animal welfare. Similarly the Association for the Repeal of the Contagious Diseases Acts had joint subscribers to its journal *The Shield* who supported temperance, feminism and moral reform (McHugh 1980). Banks (1981) has pointed out that, while there were differences in emphasis, British and American women at this period formed transatlantic links, exchanging visits and attending rallies and conventions. 'By the end of the nineteenth century, the feminist movement was based on a notion of female superiority' (Banks 1981: 84).

This trend had grown during the previous hundred years in the USA and Britain as women had engaged increasingly in the public sphere, but in a confined section and in certain specific duties. These were focused on remoralizing society through professional and philanthropic work and in areas such as education. Conceptually, the basis for this lay in notions of 'separate spheres' for men and women, which led, especially in areas of public morality, to a neat paradox. If women (as many anti-suffragists believed) were weak, frail and different and thus unable to vote or hold office, then their frailty needed guidance and protection from members of their own sex. There was also a growing culture of 'true woman-hood' which emphasized women's virtues of love, gentleness and high purity (Banks 1981: 86). Originally offered by men such as John Ruskin to justify keeping women in domesticity, it was exploited by women like Frances Willard, founder of the WCTU, to justify the belief that females were God's chosen apostles of reform. This doctrine was effectively used in the late nineteenth century campaigns and was a key feature of those which led to the entry of women into policing.

European women engaged in these activities and around the same shared concerns. Even though there were real constraints on their actions – on the public political participation of women in Germany for instance – nevertheless 'between 1885 and 1933 middle-class women social reformers in the United States and Germany conducted a transatlantic dialogue that explored each other's political cultures' (Sklar *et al.* 1998: 1).

The world's first policewoman was appointed in Stuttgart in 1903 and one of the very first international comparative studies of policing undertaken and published anywhere covered what were then the German-speaking countries of Europe. In 1910 the National Women's Council of the Netherlands commissioned Cornelia Beaujon to undertake a survey and produce a report on the work of women in policing. She sent a questionnaire to all European cities that she knew employed policewomen, received twenty-one replies and visited sixteen cities, presenting her find-ings in tabulated, spreadsheet format. Although she consciously restricted herself to German-speaking countries for practical reasons, Beaujon emphasized the transnational nature of what she was studying and set out 'general principles' (Beaujon 1911: 93) which should be universally applied to the employment of policewomen. One of the many ironies of this pioneering (and untranslated) study is that in 1911 she grouped together police-women from sixteen 'Germanic' cities in Austria, Germany and Switzerland, presenting a transEuropean phenomenon. With the many shifts in frontiers of the twentieth century they can now be found in Russia and Poland as well.

Australia and New Zealand's histories are not as yet as fully researched as those of the northern hemisphere, although there is evidence of clear links and parallels: Adela Pankhurst, youngest daughter of Emmeline, the British suffragette leader, emigrated to Australia. Almost 100 years earlier, Jane Franklin had made the same voyage and in 1843 started the Tasmanian Society for the Reformation of Female Prisoners, following the example of Elizabeth Fry, with whom she corresponded on the topic. The Women's Christian Temperance Union flourished in New Zealand and, under the leadership of Kate Sheppard, was linked more closely to the franchise campaigns there in the 1880s than in Britain. The accounts of the movements in both countries show the same phenomena of overlapping membership and linkages as well as, given the much greater distances involved and the difficulties of travel, a remarkable degree of international contact.

What, however, is distinctive in Australia and New Zealand is that women were enfranchised much earlier than in Britain and the USA. White Australian women were the first female 'citizens in the world to gain full political rights . . . the right to vote and stand for election to their national parliament' (Lake 1998: 223). New Zealand granted women the vote in 1894, but not, at first, the right to stand as Members of Parliament. The effects of this were striking and long lasting:

> In the post-suffrage decades [in Australia] women's rights and reform organizations proliferated, and the feminist as amateur politician or activist citizen came into her own . . . hence the crusade against vice, the central demand of raising the age of consent, the alarms about white slavery, the insistence that women be appointed to all public offices charged with the welfare of women and girls.
>
> (Lake 1998: 224–5)

In New Zealand too,

> for the activists in the women's movement, the franchise was a beginning rather than an end. The vote was a first step in a wider feminist agenda, which sought to bring equality between the sexes by challenging male prerogatives.
>
> (Brooks 1993: 140)

Much of the agenda promoted by women's movements during this era was close to that of the pre-suffrage era and indeed some of the organizations such as the WCTU were still flourishing. In addition, very specific conditions coincided so that it became

> part of the Australian political tradition to look to the state for a response to social issues. Australia's nation building took place during a period when social liberalism was on the ascent in the United Kingdom. The concept of the state as a vehicle for social justice . . . has been embodied in the state experiments of Australia and New Zealand since the 1890s. Distinctive Australasian institutions were created at this time.
>
> (Sawer 1995: 23–4)

A particular consequence was that, while women's movements of all types flourished in post-suffrage Australia, they focused much of their activity on

> a continuation of nineteenth century feminist preoccupations . . . the important difference [was] that the advent of citizenship and Australian feminists' close identification with the new nation-state encouraged them to formulate their claims as claims on the State.
>
> (Lake 1998: 225–6)

A much later twentieth century development which followed on from these was the appearance of 'femocrats' in Australia (Yeatman 1990), a theme to which we shall return.

pioneer policewomen and international movements

Within five years of each other, the first policewomen were appointed in the USA (in 1910), Australia and Britain (both in 1915). There were many shared characteristics in both their designated roles, the reasons for their recruitment and the pressures which led to this outcome. The exact histories for each nation can be found in Schulz (1995) for the USA, Lock (1979) for Britain and Prenzler (1994) for Australia; each story has its own characteristics and variations. The British struggle for women's entry was the longest – women were not given full statutory recognition there until 1931 – and the campaign is the only one to have prompted an entire scholarly study (Carrier 1988). Nevertheless, all three countries manifest enough common aspects for this to be worthy of remark, as Prenzler (1994: 78) puts it: 'The participation of women in policing has been part of a pattern common to Western countries'.

The common threads include

- a focus on social and welfare work
- well educated recruits from middle- or upper-class backgrounds
- an external 'policewomen's movement' which played a part in women's entry.

All the early officers fulfilled specialist roles, working with female and juvenile offenders and victims and focusing on protection. This trend was most marked in the USA, where the first policewomen carried no weapons, did not wear uniforms and carried out mainly protective duties. Schulz (1995: 43) points out that when Alice Stebbins Wells, the first US woman officer, and her colleagues decided to form their own association, they did so under the auspices of the National Conference of Social Work and that they continued to schedule their annual conferences together. British policewomen shared many of the same roots with their US counterparts, but they did wear uniforms of a kind as soon as they could; they also pursued the aim of welfare and protective work, even though the nature of their remit was a matter of controversy between some of the earliest pioneers. There was indeed a significant split among them over this (Carrier 1988).

Australia's first policewomen came into law enforcement with the same objectives. In New South Wales Kate Cocks, Australia's first policewoman, had equal powers of arrest with her male colleagues, but her responsibilities were for female offenders and welfare work with women and children. Prenzler summarizes these early years by observing that 'women were used to fill a gap between law enforcement and welfare, and to mitigate difficulties experienced by policemen in managing female offenders and female victims of crime' (Prenzler 1994: 88).

In all three countries, the first women officers and their successors for many years to come were older, well educated and often came from another, caring profession. Alice Stebbins Wells had a theology degree, had run a small church and was a welfare worker in Los Angeles, while Kate Cocks was a teacher and probation officer. Giving evidence in Britain in 1921 to the Baird Committee on the Employment of Women on Police Duties, Margaret Damer Dawson, Commandant of the Women Police Service (the more radical and ultimately unsuccessful body) claimed that her organization had recruited mainly well educated women – 669 had training, 411 had none – and many had private means: '130 were nurses, 75 were teachers' (Baird Committee 1921: 59, §1010–12). Of their US counterparts, Schulz (1995: 4) comments: 'The policewomen who served from 1910 until the post-Depression years were . . . usually upper-middle class, native born college educated social workers'.

Finally, all three sets of pioneers were encouraged, supported and indeed brought into being by groups which formed policewomen's movements. These took varied forms but all had their roots in, or were closely allied to, the range of purity and moral reform organizations described in the previous section, all of which had originally lobbied and agitated for matrons in prisons to guard and protect girls and women. In Victoria, the National Council of Women agitated for seven years before 'women warders [were] appointed to Melbourne police lockups in 1909' (Prenzler 1994: 81). Queensland offers the most interesting case in this regard, since it was the last state in Australia to recruit policewomen and did so only after considerable lobbying, which had begun in 1911, by a range of women's organizations. The National Council of Women of Queensland initiated public campaigns in 1915 which failed, and these escalated again in the late 1920s, when a coalition of women's groups and the Catholic Archbishop of Brisbane promoted the cause. The crucial event was the election in 1929 of Irene Longman, the first woman MP in Queensland. She supported the case and persuaded the government (Prenzler 1998: 4).

The twenty year campaign in Britain was also supported by alliances of the great and the good – high status women (and men) and many women's organizations. These were particularly powerful and resourceful, as they needed to be, since the initial 'experiments' of women patrols during the First World War had taken considerable drive to achieve and then these were threatened in 1922 by budgetary cuts. Quite remarkable resources and tactics were deployed by key proponents, including Nancy

Astor (the first woman MP to take her seat at Westminster) and several peers in the Lords (Carrier 1988: 122–4) and there was regular lobbying then and during the 1920s by formidable alliances of the movement which even had its own journal, *The Policewoman's Review*, which promoted the cause.

Schulz (1995) also notes the importance of these sources of support for the policewomen in early twentieth century USA. In particular, she draws attention to the distinctive American phenomenon of women's clubs. By the 1920s these clubs had a membership of well over a million women who shared a 'Progressive, child-saver philosophy dominated by college-educated, middle class women' (Schulz 1995: 50). These clubs and their federation provided structures and an institutional voice for women to express a role in political life. The 'interlocking directorates' enabled cross-support for each other's causes, of which the entry of women into policing was a key one (Blair 1980; Schulz 1995).

While there were significant local differences, it can be persuasively argued that the early days of the pioneer policewomen in English-speaking and some European countries had much in common with each other and formed a very distinct phenomenon within policing in each nation. One of the main reasons for this was that an international policewomen's movement existed which linked those promoting and supporting the movement, and later those who entered it. Rupp (1994), focusing on three of the major women's organizations at the turn of the nineteenth century, has stressed how these large, diverse groups of women 'organized transnationally and *struggled to define* a group identity in a period marked by two global conflagrations' (Rupp 1994: 1572, emphasis added). She argues that they engaged in a deliberate and constant process:

> The international collective identity that was created and sustained within these organizations – the boundaries, the consciousness of internationalism and the politicization of everyday life – served as the glue that held together these diverse women.
>
> (Rupp 1994: 1598–9)

She suggests one reason for the attraction of

> international collective identity [which] held the potential
> for wider appeal . . . women could unite through . . . the
> reality of worldwide violence against women.
>
> (Rupp 1994: 1599)

For those women who promoted the role of women in law enforcement, transnationalism was central to their campaigns in many
other ways too and we return to this below. First, we consider how
these links and the concept of the international policewoman
were constructed.

international alliances

We have suggested that there was an international movement for
policewomen in the *fin de siècle* era; it would perhaps be more
accurate to say that support for women's entry into policing was
a key cause linked to a whole set of concerns for women of this
period. It was a common thread running through female networks
such as those with moral and religious aims such as temperance
as well as supporters of social justice and emancipation. A very
diverse coalition of groups and individuals came to believe that
attested officer status would enable women involved in welfare
and rescue work to carry it out more effectively.

How these ideas came to have such widespread acceptance is
beyond the scope of this chapter (we address some of the issues
in Brown and Heidensohn 2000). For present purposes it is important to stress that the struggle for the vote in all three countries
was related to new ways of looking at the state and its powers in
the lives of women. We have already noted Australia's distinctive
history with female enfranchisement *preceding* and stimulating
the growth of women's organizations which engaged directly with
the state and policy making, ultimately leading to the appearance
of femocrats in the 1970s who entered government to promote
feminist interests from within. Questions of polity were very different in Britain and the USA but in both nations women sought
formal powers and roles in law enforcement as part of wider social
and political projects.

The best illustration perhaps of the ways in which these older
alliances worked is to outline some of the key transatlantic (and
indeed wider) links which influenced British and US policing in

their earliest days. When Margaret Damer Dawson and Mary Allen first approached the British Home Office about setting up women's patrols at the outbreak of the First World War, they were able to back their claim with reference to the experience of other countries, including the USA and Denmark. Damer Dawson in her evidence to the Baird Committee mentioned her earlier work: 'on the Continent in previous years with regard to the white slave traffic' (Baird Committee 1921: 54, §905) and the International Bureau for the Suppression of the White Slave Trade had held its conference in London in July 1913; among the resolutions passed there was one on the need for the appointment of policewomen in order to control the 'evil trade'.

After the First World War was over American born MP Nancy Astor was both tireless in promoting the role of policewomen in Britain (Carrier 1988) and also in the USA where she helped to fund the International Association of Policewomen (IAP) and served as its first chair; when the future of the women patrols was in doubt at the end of the war she invited Minna Van Winkle, president of the IAP, to England to speak on their behalf (Schulz 1995: 53).

The IAP had been founded in 1915 and began with and retained close ties with social work and the American Social Hygiene Association. Its title was perhaps optimistic since Damer Dawson was the only founder member from outside North America. Nevertheless, transatlantic links did develop in the 1920s and Mary Allen visited the USA in 1924 as a guest of the League of Women Voters, lecturing and meeting policewomen as well as directing the traffic in New York (Carrier 1988).

In 1923 Allen went to Cologne, where the British Armies were occupying the Rhineland, with a small party of six women officers to provide a protective service for young girls. The spur to this female force had been the visit of Mrs Corbett Ashby, Secretary of the International Women's Suffrage Alliance, to Germany where she had been horrified by 'vice, disease and crime' she saw there (Lock 1979: 146). Even after the British Army withdrew, links were maintained with the Women Police Service and German women recruited in Cologne.

Throughout the 1920s and 1930s *The Policewoman's Review*, published by Allen and her supporters, reported on international visits and links, producing accounts of the work of policewomen in Germany, Sweden, Sydney and the USA. Some of these are self-congratulatory – in 1934 an anniversary edition celebrated ten years since the Cologne experiment – but they do provide a considerable record of a project under construction, the international policewomen movement.

The skills with which Allen and her colleagues sustained and developed the idea are remarkable and resemble those of present-day spin doctors. *The Policewoman's Review* was regularly filled with international material, especially photographs, which were quite often recycled, but there was also a stress on the most modern technologies of the day and how policewomen were (or would soon be) at the forefront of its application to policing on a worldwide basis. In July 1931 the front cover pictured Mrs Ulysses G. McQueen (*sic*) 'the first air policewoman in the world' and deftly managed to introduce, in four short paragraphs, references to the USA, France, Europe, England, Switzerland, Germany and Jerusalem (*The Policewoman's Review*, July 1931, vol. V, no. 3). In 1934 'Commandant' Mary Allen was reported as taking to the air herself on a series of visits to European policewomen.

The *Review* nevertheless recorded official activities which took place and supported the 'cause' of policewomen. An article in the first issue outlined the purpose of the International Committee for Women Police (*The Policewoman's Review*, May 1927, vol. 1, no. 1). Another article in May 1932 covered the same committee and noted that it now had affiliates from thirty-four countries and links to the League of Nations. Its role in furthering the role of women in policing was also noted (*The Policewoman's Review*, October 1927, vol. 1, no. 6).

At the same time in the USA, the IAP recorded the association's development and what Schulz (1995: 54) described as 'the decline of the policewomen's movement' in its *Policewoman's International Bulletin*. Schulz ascribed the demise of the IAP in 1936 to two sets of factors, one to do with the changing nature of feminism and women's organizations, the second to the developments in American policing. She described feminism as losing momentum after 1925, with women's associations declining and very few new ones being formed. 'Another reason for the decline of the movement and the IAP itself, was the decline of the temperance and reformist groups that had been the major advocates for policewomen' (Schulz 1995: 55). The very sources of earlier strength and support turned to weakness both because they themselves faded away, but also because of changes in policing itself.

Schulz argues that the pioneers' acceptance of separate spheres for men and women in policing and hence a restricted 'feminine' role for women was nearly fatal. American policing was professionalized and militarized in the 1920s and 1930s. Women were seen as marginal and irrelevant. The IAP and policewomen's movement had preferred to stay close to female supporters outside the police who rejected many aspects of newstyle, militaristic law enforcement. Notably, the Americans had been appalled by the spectacle of the uniforms worn by the British women and had openly criticized them and some of the British and European approach (Lock 1979). Above all, the international movement was *external* to police organizations and could not exercise effective influence upon them.

There were other reasons for the decline of women's international organizations at this period. The First World War had seen nationalism rise and flourish all over Europe – British suffrage campaigners ceased their struggle during the war and worked, in many cases, for the war effort. A few women remained pacifist and internationalist in outlook (Wiltsher 1985) on both sides and continued with many new and revived projects afterwards. But with the Depression and the rise of fascism in Europe this grew increasingly difficult (Sklar *et al.* 1998). The first 'global' networks formed by women had great strength of vision and considerable support. When a key cause, such as the policewomen movement, became central it was promoted and supported tirelessly by well connected and skilled operators, who were often wealthy and also well connected. But the leadership consisted of only a few people, often independent minded and sometimes too highly individual to work well with others or within organizations (Britain's pioneer history was marked by 'turf' wars between competing groups). While initially it was a strength to have bases and support *outside* the police, the failure to move on from this position was ultimately a weakness.

There were other limits on international links: no real agreement existed on the appropriate role for women in policing. Within each nation there were often differences; across the world there were many more. Americans maintained their attachment to a non-uniformed, welfare role longer and more strongly than did the British and, to some extent, the Australians. In several European countries, policewomen stayed in this position or an even narrower one for a long time. Swedish 'police sisters' maintained their function for twenty-five years, Germany experienced 'missions' of British officers after both world wars and saw prolonged debates and some scandals about the work of their own policewomen (Fairchild 1987). Finally, what we might call the tides of history did not always run favourably during the twentieth century. Women in general and in policing made considerable political and related gains in the first two twentieth century decades. The Depression and fascism had very negative effects and in both the USA and UK only the Second World War restored some of the previous gains.

future parallels

In the modern era three alliances have been set up to promote the interests of women in policing. In 1956 the International Association of Women Police (IAWP) was founded in the USA, in 1989 the European Network of Policewomen (ENP) was set up in the Netherlands and in 1997, the Australasian Council of Women and Policing (ACWAP) was incorporated. The modern networks differ in structures and objectives, although their broad aims are similar. The IAWP is a membership organization which is organized regionally and, though growing more broadly based, is mainly confined to the USA and Canada. Nevertheless, it has increasingly set out to reach women in other countries and has instituted awards for them. In 1996, the IAWP held its annual conference outside North America for the first time and did so jointly with ENP. In 1998 the ENP executive attended the IAWP congress in Alaska, and in 1999 the IAWP travelled to Europe to hold its board meeting at the ENP conference (Schulz 1998; European Network of Policewomen 1999).

ENP was instituted at a conference held in the Netherlands in 1989 and, while sponsored by the Dutch government, was explicitly and intentionally international from the outset. Its transnational role is particularly interesting since, based in Europe and in the middle of Schengenland, it is at the heart of the growth area for transnational policing. ENP is itself a small organization which promotes and supports the setting up of national networks in European countries and provides links between them through its newsletter, conferences and seminars. ENP was represented at the second Australasian Conference on Women and Policing in

1999. ACWAP is a more fledgling alliance than the others, but is notable for having as its third key aim 'Creating an Australasian link in the global network of women in policing'.

The IAWP has become much more broadly based in worldwide membership, but is still American run and dominated (Schulz, 1998). The ENP, as a government sponsored rather than a membership organization, has been international in outlook from its inception and its Dutch board deliberately stood down in 1995 to be replaced by an international one. Schulz (1998: 79) argues that the ENP 'is better positioned to become an international voice for women in policing than the IAWP', partly because the latter has become a social forum and has a poor and conservative record on backing change and developments in women's role. IAWP, for instance, continued to support separate women's bureaux until the 1970s.

The pioneers of policing for women had to construct an international dimension to their cause in order for it to succeed. At a very simple level they were able to *validate* their claims to enter this male preserve by reference to the experience of other countries – the argument from good example and good practice. The British pioneers regularly did so and this remains a powerful persuasion up to the present. ACWAP invited contributors from Europe to its 1999 conference to outline the setting up of global networks. Another feature of the pioneers' case was their *universalizing* of the problems for which they saw policewomen as *the* solution: essentially these were 'vice', trafficking in women and abuse of children. Again, the contemporary organizations still stress a common, universal agenda, although it is now domestic violence, trafficking and child abuse. Interestingly, the global problem which is now likely to concern women in law enforcement is the harassment and discrimination they experience from male colleagues (Brown and Heidensohn 2000). Linking internationally is one way to achieve a *critical mass* of colleagues with whom one can network, gain support and build resistance to abuse. This was brought home to us in the interviews we undertook with delegates to the 1996 IAWP/ENP Conference in Birmingham (see Chapter 5). Several stressed their isolation in their own agencies and said how conferences provided alternatives to traditional police cultures. Finally, policewomen developed their project internationally because of the reluctance of national governments to accept them: the British government was incensed at the skilful way in which Mary Allen manipulated the American press during her visit there. Many of the reasons for constructing a global project of women in policing remain relevant today: percentages of women are still fairly small – 25 per cent is the highest (in Stockholm and Detroit) – and it is under 20 per cent in the UK and around 10 per cent in the USA. Promotion and deployment are often restricted.

There are grounds for confidence in the future of the existing alliances and, possibly, for the growth of others. A range of factors likely to favour further growth of transnationalism in women's role in policing are set out below:

- changes in policing
- transnational policing (for example Europol)
- democratic transformations (for example Eastern Europe and South Africa)
- demilitarization of police (for example new democracies and Northern Ireland)
- networks inside the police
- resources
- rise of femocrats.

changes in policing

These changes include the growth of professionalism and specialization as well as pressures for greater accountability, crackdown on corruption and stress on new agendas for the police. On the whole such changes benefit women, who gain from meritocratic selection and from a lesser emphasis on brute force, and a switch to community policing and less confrontational styles of policing. Such trends tend to be rapidly 'globalized' now and will be increasingly so (see Chan 1997).

transnational policing

In some parts of the world, most notably in the European Union, transnational policing is developing, with forces cooperating across frontiers. One effect of this process, an intended outcome of the implementation of the Maastricht Treaty of 1991, is co-ordination and some standardization. While this may not lead to harmony, it does lead to some growing internationalism, for example English police in Kent and their French counterparts have developed a communication system in order to police the Channel Tunnel and its environs (Heidensohn 1996a).

democratic transformations

The rise of facism in Europe destroyed earlier international bodies such as the League of Nations and its affiliations. The demise of communism in Eastern Europe in the 1980s and 1990s has, however, encouraged international alliances and enabled specific links and projects to go ahead. Opening up policing in a more liberal way, including the recruitment of women, has been actively pursued. In South Africa, issues of domestic violence and sexual assault have been tackled, as well as those of more public and political violence.

demilitarization of police

As well as general democratization of many countries there have been specific projects to demilitarize the police in several countries and/or specific agencies. The most recent and notable example is the Royal Ulster Constabulary in Northern Ireland where the Patten Commission proposed innovative solutions.

networks inside the police

The modern networks of IAWP, ENP and the Australasian Council are inside the police and/or close to or accepted by police; they are not outside bodies funding alternatives.

resources

In some instances, at least, resources have been made available to fund networks and similar initiatives. ENP is subsidized by the Dutch government and by other European governments in cash or in kind. The Swedish government paid for network coordinators to be trained and to develop networks there.

rise of femocrats

In the 1920s the presence of a sole female MP could ensure that the cause of policewomen was promoted. In the twenty-first century there are femocrats and many more female politicians and policy makers who can influence outcomes much more systematically. They are credited with playing a much more significant role in Australia and the USA in recent times than in the UK (Stetson and Mazur 1995). It will be interesting to see if this changes in twenty-first century Britain.

advice and warnings

Pioneers in the policewomen's movement did not always share common purposes: their conceptions of the role of women in policing were diverse and sometimes contradictory. Schulz (1998) has pointed out that there are contemporary parallels to the earlier debates around separate spheres. In India, Pakistan and some parts of Central and South America, women-only stations have been set up in order to provide refuge and support for female victims. Too much diversity can dilute effort and lead to confusion; generally there does seem very widespread agreement on the role of policewomen as uniformed, integrated officers.

Blueprints for new networks ought to have issues highlighted in three areas:

- networks and support
- power points and femocrats
- organizations.

networks and support

We have already stressed the advantages of having networks based within or inside the police. However, we also wish to stress the need for *external* support and alliances. These may take the form of links with community or involvements with the media and with pressure groups. The modern police have in general become very sophisticated users of the media (Innes 1999) although they can occasionally be foolish or crass (Chan 1997). In general, stories about international female alliances in policing will be 'good' stories. Other groups who may prove helpful allies are researchers and academics and pressure groups with like interests.

power points and femocrats

Global and local networks (it hardly requires stressing) need to be
plugged into the mains, connected with the major power centres
of government police hierarchies, trade unions, quangos, and so
on. The close liaison in the Netherlands between ENP and its
sponsor department has been crucial. Femocrats may operate as
individuals and networks need links with them too to ensure
that key changes are made.

organizations

Networks need regular attention given to their purposes and
structures. ENP has proved something of a model in this regard,
regularly reviewing its plans and mission and updating them.
IAWP, however, stayed for too long with an outmoded model
for policewomen (Schulz 1998). Obviously, too, such bodies need
resources; the IAP faded with its diminished funding. The IAP
and the other parts of the policewomen's movement were led by
formidable women who often had charisma, but were not always
adapted to everyday bureaucracy. Nowadays charisma needs to
be routinized, so that networks do not depend solely on powerful
personalities, and sometimes, their money.

The pictures and stories of the first policewomen and their
supporters leap from past pages of bulletins and reviews. They
sparked radical changes in women policing and the policing of
women. They were missionaries in blue, determined to protect
their own sex and sometimes to control. They believed in global
networks, which they used effectively and creatively for their
cause. Today's purposes are different, but the parallels are great.
The pioneers all got their chances in times of upheaval or of war
(in Britain and Australia). The opportunities offered in the new
millennium are much more promising, but it is salutary to recollect
how inauspicious were the bars, brothels, parks and munitions
factories where the first patrols went and how much they made
of those opportunities.

note on research material

In preparing this chapter we have drawn on several sources of
primary material in addition to scholarly and official accounts.

We conducted a survey of 804 serving female officers from thirty-five countries in 1996–7 (see Brown and Heidensohn (2000) for an account and analysis). We have also attended conferences and meetings held by all three of the contemporary organizations for policewomen, often giving papers or addresses. We have used reports, bulletins, newsletters and conference programmes from the respective organizations. In 1996, we interviewed policewomen at the first joint International Congress of Policewomen held in Birmingham in England (see Heidensohn 1997b; Brown and Heidensohn 2000; Chapter 5).

We consulted archive material at the Public Records Office at Kew, Bramshill Police College library, the Imperial War Museum and the Metropolitan Police Museum.

Finally, Frances Heidensohn interviewed key personnel of the European Network of Policewomen in the Netherlands and other member countries, including Austria, Sweden, Germany, Hungary and Britain in 1996 and 1997.

sisters, strangers and serendipity:
research on gender in a postmodern setting

Accounts of carrying out research often stress the problems encountered in undertaking the project. This is a departure from some earlier practice, as Brewer has pointed out:

> ethnographers of the police largely have been silent on the difficulties they encountered, implying that their entry into the field and relations with police officers were unproblematic.
> (Brewer 1990a: 579)

In more recent times there have been several descriptions of such problems, some of them having serious impact on the outcomes of the study (for example Van Maanen 1988; Punch 1989). Brewer himself has provided some of the most thoughtful and nuanced analyses of the difficulties he faced, and the solutions he devised (and their cost) when carrying out a study of the Royal Ulster Constabulary (Brewer 1990a, 1990b, 1991).

One of the undoubted reasons for the fuller, more honest descriptions which are now much more characteristic of social researchers' presentations of their methods is the impact of feminism. As Oakley succinctly puts it, the conclusion of a mass of critiques, evaluations and debates is that 'methodology is itself gendered' (Oakley 1998: 707). This view has led to detailed consideration of the research process: the notion that it is a detached, risk-free enterprise has been rejected (Reinharz 1984) and major approaches have been avoided because they lead to inequality in power relations (Acker *et al*. 1991) or they do not serve feminism well (Smith 1989). A notable effect of such debates has been that scholars, and not only feminist scholars, recount their adventures and misadventures in research in a more direct, almost confessional way (see for example Porter 1996).

This shift may be less apparent in criminology and work on crime and justice, not least perhaps because this is still a very male-dominated field: 80 per cent of the respondents to Rock's (1994) surveys of the profession were male (although I am not of course claiming that no man can be feminist, nor that all women are). Nevertheless, even this most machismo-dominated area of social science has undergone some changes and has seen the publication of a set of accounts by established criminologists of the growth of their research and theoretical perspectives:

> in this book academic criminologists have written about the intertwining of personal lives and intellectual pursuits. *Ours is a confessional culture.*
>
> (Holdaway and Rock 1998: 175, added emphasis)

The following account is intended to add to this growing literature and debate. First of all it is a report of a successful attempt to solve a research problem, that of obtaining a 'thick' (i.e. qualitatively rich) and a varied sample of female officers for an international, comparative project, all of whom could be interviewed to provide qualitative data. At this level it adds to the range of what might be called 'recipe' collections of how to carry out a research study, especially what one might call the 'starter' part of the menu, where gaining access and developing rapport are emphasized. For two thoughtful and very different reflections on this process in police research see Hunt (1984) and Reiner (1992: ch. 3); as I have already suggested, such positive accounts can be compared with those where only limited access was achieved, or where negotiations led to pragmatic compromises having to be made (for the latter see Brewer 1990a, 1990b, 1991; Shaw 1998).

In addition, I hope that this account contributes to and draws together two themes in recent discussions of methodological questions. On the one hand is the large and complex area of feminist epistemology which flourishes most at philosophical and theoretical heights, although there are points of intersection with empirical and policy-related work (for examples see Daly 1994, 1998). On the other hand are those introductions to research studies, especially those on crime and criminal justice subjects, which while reflecting on this process, do not engage with the wider issues raised by the feminist critique (for instance Hobbs 1995). This chapter is intended as a modest attempt at integrating these approaches.

First, I outline the project and how its aims were achieved; later in the chapter I highlight the aspects of this account which seem the most significant and relevant for consideration in wider debates. These are questions of *access*, *relationships* with subjects and *observations* of their actions and interactions. Finally, I suggest that a conference is a distinctive and notable site for research and that it constitutes a *postmodern setting* in which to observe and record.

research on gender in a postmodern setting

The purpose of this section is to report on using an international conference of police officers as a research site and as the source of a series of interviewees. As far as I have been able to ascertain, there are no comparable reports in the literature and thus one intention behind this account is to locate others and make comparisons.[1] Some important and expected benefits flowed from exploiting the opportunity which this event offered: these consisted chiefly in gaining *access*

* to an international sample, gathered in one place at one time
* to a group of criminal justice professionals who can prove elusive and to whom access is not always officially available.

In addition there were extras which developed in this particular situation, including observing

* ceremonial dramas, played out as part of the conventional rituals
* social processes and interactions between delegates
* the ways in which the convention centre's public/private space boundaries were (re)constructed by the delegates.

All of these aided and enhanced the projects which my colleagues and I were undertaking. Some problems did emerge during the conference, but these did not outweigh the considerable advantages. I set out below a brief outline of the background to the project, cite some examples of the 'added value' material we were able to gather and conclude with a discussion of the conference as a research site for criminologists, especially in the light of key developments in the privatization of public space and with some reflections on the reflexivity of researchers.

the projects and the background

The projects served by this enterprise are two studies of the role of women in law enforcement in international and comparative perspective. The first, jointly undertaken by Dr Jennifer Brown and myself, but very much led and inspired by her, arose from Jenny Brown's work on equal opportunities for women in policing (Brown and Campbell 1991; Brown 1997). Initially we had sent a questionnaire to women officers in various countries which elicited considerable data on their experiences of discrimination, deployment and harassment. This had already yielded a considerable amount of valuable material, albeit from a short and relatively simply designed questionnaire. When we learned that the first joint congress of the two international organizations for policewomen would take place in Birmingham, England, in 1996, we decided that this would provide an unrepeatable opportunity to add interviews with officers drawn from a wide range of countries.[2] In addition to my involvement in this study, I was planning research on networking for and by women in law enforcement and with an especial focus on the European Network of Policewomen, one of the organizations mounting the conference. Thus I was interested in interviewing participants on their own experiences of networking, in observing the ENP activities due to take place at the conference and in making contacts with ENP members in European countries whom I intended to visit in the coming year.[3] There are several personal background features of both of the principal researchers which I should emphasize, first to give depth to this account and also because these were later to be of some relevance in various interactions and encounters during the conference.

Both Jenny Brown and I had conducted previous studies of women and policing (Heidensohn 1989; Brown and Campbell 1991; Coffey *et al.* 1992; Heidensohn 1992, 1994b; Brown *et al.* 1995). These had largely been published in conventional academic forms as research reports, books and journal articles, but we had also been interviewed by the media when, for instance, cases of harassment or discrimination were publicized or when the first woman chief constable in the UK was appointed. We had spoken to professional criminal justice audiences about our research findings, notably at the 1994 ENP conference in Brussels and in July 1996 in Sydney at the first Australasian Conference on Women in Policing. Finally, we had advised on and been interviewed for a British TV documentary *Service with a Smile* (directed by Rosalind Haber for Cactus Films, 1994) which has been widely shown. In short, we had some familiarity with the topics we were studying, while we were also known to some of those we wished to interview and observe. We were both asked to contribute to the event as speakers.

Reiner (1991: 46–51) points out the consequences of having become relatively well known as a police researcher when he was interviewing chief constables. He notes that several of his subjects had read his work and this both formed their views of him and led them to engage in discussion, and sometimes to attempt rebuttal, during their interviews. As he observes: '"Presumptions and preconceptions" are of course written into all research, and also into the reception of the researcher by respondents' (Reiner 1991: 49). So far as we could tell, the presumptions and preconceptions about us in our research role were relatively favourable. Following my appearance on the opening day of the conference on a panel devoted to the topic of 'Shattering the Glass Ceiling', I was approached by an officer from the USA whom I had interviewed for my earlier comparative work (Heidensohn 1992), who greeted me warmly, evidently pleased by that study.

Of course there is an opposite danger to what might be called failure of access due to mistrust: the problem of the tame or naïve researcher, one who may be regarded as too gullible or easily incorporated into the institution he or she is studying. Although the police themselves may regard liberal academic researchers as hostile and anti-police (Smith and Gray 1981; Reiner 1991) and at least one academic has castigated his colleagues for this (Waddington 1999: 292), there are examples of investigators who have confessed that they became too close to the police (Punch 1989) and thus had their results affected. In this study, which was not based solely on an ethnographic observation of a single site, nor confined to interviews with officers from one force, or even one country, such a risk seems much less likely. We would acknowledge, however, that it was our contacts and our profiles as researchers which gained us entrée and also permission to approach and interview conference delegates. It is worth noting that, in 1992, my request to attend the Bramshill Conference on 'Quality through Equality', which was the second bi-annual event organized by the ENP, was turned down. (A full account of the research referred to here including an analysis of the interviews undertaken at the conference can be found in Brown and Heidensohn 2000.)

planning and improvising

Since the event was scheduled to last only five days we realized at an early stage that we should have to plan carefully in order to achieve at least our minimum aim of over twenty interviews. At the same time, we recognized that our approach had to be highly flexible and 'opportunistic' in the fullest sense in order to take advantage of interview opportunities as they arose. It was clear that we would need assistance and we were fortunately able to recruit three additional interviewers, two of whom were graduate students of mine and the third then a colleague of Jenny's.[4] All had relevant previous experience and had interviewed police officers. We held a series of planning meetings during the earlier months of 1996 and devised a strategy to take maximum advantage of the opportunity offered by the conference. This included

- producing publicity material (to be mailed to delegates) identifying us all as the 'research roadshow'
- liaising with the conference organizers to ensure facilities
- setting up an introduction party for the first evening to which we invited potential interviewees.

We also developed interview checklists, cover sheets and a series of targets for interviewees from different countries and regions which we aimed to achieve. For instance, we were especially keen to contact and interview officers from areas which are normally hard to reach and/or those on which little or no research material has been published. Thus we planned to target African and Asian delegates and those from Eastern Europe. These also overlapped with another focus, namely officers from nations or forces with small percentages of women in their ranks where achieving a sample of any size would be extremely difficult. Younger women were also a priority.

In the weeks before the conference we held training and briefing sessions in London where we rehearsed the interview schedule, discussed practical details (such as battery versus mains-powered tape recorders). Contact was maintained with the organizers.

the conference: background

Publicity material for the conference described it as the 'International Police Training Conference' and gave its organizers as the International Association of Women Police 'in co-operation with' the European Network for Policewomen. IAWP, stated this brochure, 'was founded in 1915 in Los Angeles, USA'. This, however, is misleading. In fact the International Association of Policewomen did originate in this way but it went into decline during the 1920s and ceased to exist in 1932, being reformed only in 1956 as the IAWP, and then having a notably different orientation from its predecessor, which had been closely associated with professional social work, rather than policing (Schulz 1995: 117).

The ENP was, on the other hand, correctly portrayed as 'established in 1989 during a Conference in the Netherlands'. The key aims of both bodies were set out in boxes of the brochure. The third sponsor, the West Midlands Police, was also listed; it and the Metropolitan Police gave considerable support to the event.

There are several issues to note here. One is the differences in approach of the two bodies – their distinctive missions, one might say. Among the most important are their structures – IAWP has a series of regions, covering the world, although it is overwhelmingly a US organization. ENP has an international secretariat, but consists of networks in most European countries. It is funded and supported by the Dutch government and receives subsidies from other European states. Further features are the cultures of the two and their membership criteria, aspects of which became more apparent during the days in Birmingham.

There is a long history of international work which promoted the participation of women in law enforcement. Indeed, such movements considerably predate the entry of women into policing and their membership was often much larger and/or their aims much grander than everyday reality. In Britain, the campaign to achieve women's entry was long drawn out (Carrier 1988), taking twenty years, from public meetings and letters in *The Times* in 1912 to the issuing of the Police (Women) Regulations on 7 October 1931. In the UK, the campaign was from its inception, remarkably international in character.

The Home Office files for the period, held at the Public Record Office in London, yield numerous examples of this. In June 1914, that is just *before* the outbreak of the First World War which provided the circumstances for the first, volunteer women patrols in 1915, the International Bureau for the Suppression of the White Slave Trade wrote to the Home Office about the resolution, passed at their International Congress in 1913 supporting the role of women police. Their telegraphic address was 'Chivalry, South West London'.

The following year, Margaret Damer Dawson, one of the pioneer figures in this field, also wrote to the Home Secretary (28 July 1915) citing the fact that in the

> USA and other countries many bodies of learned and influential women interested in the protection and development of women police have written and spoken theoretically on the necessity for a trained body of women.

When she and her colleague, Mary Allen, were finally invited to meet the Home Secretary on 13 March 1916 they referred to experiences of employing policewomen in the USA, the Netherlands and Denmark.

The first policewomen in Europe had been appointed in Germany in the early 1900s and were widespread enough by 1911 for a PhD thesis to be written upon them (Beaujon 1911). After the defeat of Germany in 1918, the role of women in law enforcement in that country was re-established under British influences and these remained crucial until Hitler centralized them during the Third Reich (Nienhaus 1992). Even after the First World

War, international bodies passed resolutions urging that women be given wider roles in policing: the League of Nations did so in 1927 (Tancred 1931).

Despite its international character, and the links between women officers in different countries, international bodies for policewomen did not achieve long term survival in the early twentieth century. In the USA, the IAP fell victim to the Depression and to 'changes in feminism after 1925 when women's groups became more conservative' (Schulz 1995: 54). In Europe, the rise of fascism and then the onset of the Second World War damaged links which had, in the case of Britain and Germany, to be re-established all over again when it came to the work of women officers (Peto 1992: 128). I have outlined elsewhere the reasons for the failure of earlier international links and for some (guarded) optimism for the future possibilities (Heidensohn 1998 and see Chapter 4). It is important to note that the Birmingham conference was the first such event ever, but that at the same time there were precedents in earlier phases of the women police movement.

Birmingham I

In this section I shall briefly outline how we went about reaching and interviewing our target group of officers. In the next, I shall record some of the serendipitous features of observing officers in this setting.[5] The first evening event was a civic reception in Birmingham's Art Gallery, where delegates and other guests, including civic dignitaries, were mingling in splendid surroundings. The registration desk had closed early so that many delegates, and some of us, had not been able to register and had no name badges. Nevertheless, it was not difficult to identify and approach likely subjects. Most were still with national or regional groups with whom they had arrived and they were expecting to be greeted. Thus for researchers they presented nearly ideal potential subjects: available, accessible, reasonably relaxed and with no other immediate engagement. Moreover, their presence at this event signalled their own interest in our research topic. Each of the research team focused on particular groups and quickly established rapport and some commitments to be interviewed later on.

As just one example of this, since I was particularly interested in finding out both about *pre-existing networks* and links between participants and also how they used this setting either to *establish* or to *reinforce* such links, I focused on several such groups. African American officers were of especial importance, both because I had investigated some of their groupings in my 1988 study and because of their positions at the intersection of race and gender. One of the features of the congress as a whole as a research site, and of the various settings in which delegates could be observed, which was apparent at once was the scope for 'performing' their roles which was provided. At the evening reception, officers were dressed very attractively in 'cocktail' or other formal wear and were assembled in rather stately, beautifully lit rooms. At other times there were parades in uniform, structured events such as plenary lectures, seminars, board meetings, lunches and dinners, as well as a range of informal opportunities. It was clear that officers could choose from a repertoire of self-presentations and that they did so, sometimes quite consciously. One officer from a European force dutifully wore her uniform to the parade, but did so with her hair worn in a loose and casual style, symbolically undermining the formal image, a choice which she said was quite deliberate. This is very much in keeping with Brewer's (1991) observations about the ways in which female officers in the RUC manage their occupational role both at work and outside it:

> the gender of policewomen in the work setting is a social construction that is interactionally accomplished in the job rather than being a simple reflection of their sex roles outside the work place.
>
> (Brewer 1991: 244)

When the formal reception ended we took a group of members to one of the main hotels and entertained them there to drinks and snacks in the bar, explaining our project and ourselves several times in the course of the evening. Important contacts were achieved at this stage: one officer, who agreed to be interviewed that night, was to promote the experience to her colleagues and to become an important recruiter for us. It became clear, too, that our emphasis during preparation on flexibility was justified: two people asked to be interviewed at once and so the two interviewers involved (N.B. and M.S.) responded and had to wait until very late evening to have dinner.

conference days

During the actual conference we endeavoured to maintain a diary so that 'interview engagements' could be kept. While we kept to our 'dates' as far as we could, some officers failed to appear or were elusive. One or two took time to agree to respond and with one national group, the team felt that they were wary of their (male) senior officer and unwilling to participate.

The high visibility/availability of officers at the first evening reception was not sustained throughout the event, as delegates attended sessions or went out on official or privately organized visits. Plans we had initially made to have our own stall or corner in the Convention Centre could not be realized as neither its design nor the space rented by the organizers lent themselves to this. However, the structure of the centre and, perhaps more importantly, the ways in which the delegates themselves used it were striking.

The Birmingham Convention Centre is a multi-storey glass and steel construction which contains Symphony Hall, an international-standard concert hall, as well as a range of lecture theatres and seminar rooms. These are all built round an arcade which runs the length and most of the height of the building and forms a passageway between two parts of the new cityscape of Birmingham – Century Square and a redeveloped area round a canal basin called Brindley Place. This was used by the public as a through way and thus delegates had to find and mark out their own territories.

We observed that some of them 'patrolled' by walking through this area, sometimes 'stopping and searching' to look for friends or colleagues. To one side of the 'street' was an area filled with tables and chairs with a café which served (rather expensive) tea, coffee and light refreshments. Here, a good deal of 'easing' went on, where groups would sit and talk, but could usually be joined by others. This whole area had a high degree of visibility, from walkways above and across it, from the pavement café or while on it. Delegates themselves used it and we also took advantage of this mini-village, waiting for subjects to interview, making direct contact, noting interactions and avoidance. The scene resembled a classic city street corner from the golden years of urban ethnography, or a village setting from the days of classic anthropology. The one major difference, and enormous advantage for us, was that the population was overwhelmingly female and engaged in law enforcement.

In these circumstances, it was not difficult to establish fieldwork rapport and to achieve results from interviewing unique to this situation. For instance, while we each had targets to aim for in numbers and types of interviewees, we encouraged interviewees to choose whom they wished to be interviewed by. Some were very clear that they preferred the younger members of the team. When two of the team separately met and interviewed delegates from a region they discovered issues that they and another member were able to develop further in another session. To take another example, I particularly aimed to explore networking among African American officers, something I had observed and recorded in an earlier study. At the reception on the first day, I approached two officers and made contact, explaining what I intended to do. Observation and regular contact by me and other team members confirmed their group activities. Having arranged to meet four of them one day for a group interview, we set ourselves up on a quiet upper walkway where for over two hours a discussion ensued around their own careers, experiences of racism, sexism and so on. The group grew as others joined and then left.

Birmingham II

As noted above, both Jenny Brown and I had taken part previously in international policewomen's conferences and were aware that some ceremonies would be involved. Jenny had, for instance, been surprised by the flags and banners she had seen at the Vancouver IAWP meeting. The Birmingham conference was marked by two events on the Sunday which were symbolic and significant for observers of police culture.

First was the opening ceremony in Symphony Hall. Officers were asked to parade in uniform and most did so. Uniform has, for female officers, even more layers of importance than for males, as well as historic and national difference. Thus US and UK officers were deeply divided for many years on the subject (Carrier 1988; Schulz 1995). British women pioneers believed profoundly in the need for uniforms, while debating the shape, style and fabric of these endlessly (Wyles 1951; Carrier 1988). American women objected to the notion until much more recently. Nowadays, as could be seen in Birmingham, female uniforms are universal and extremely diverse. From straightforwardly unisex (USA) to more exotic garb, the officers were clearly taking great pride in their appearance. Some presented themselves in glamorous, feminine fashion, with long hair, make-up and (discreet) jewellery. Aspects of the ceremony had a quasi-military aspect, complete with drum rolls. We noted that the police band, drawn from the West Midlands Constabulary, the host force, were perfectly politically correct with a female drummer, an African Caribbean (male) officer and two white males.

The second notable ceremony of that day was the awards lunch. This was a lengthy, sit-down meal at which the annual awards made by the IAWP and one such by ENP were distributed. The IAWP awards recognized contributions by US colleagues, with a special one for an officer from overseas, and each one was accompanied by an elaborate citation, together with letters of support, approbation and sometimes family affection for the winners. In at least one case, tape recordings were used to illustrate the events. Other recipients were accompanied by relatives who were at the ceremony. It was in marked contrast to the morning's formal quasi-military style; it was a highly emotional session and, to us as observers, seemed *designedly* so. The audience were encouraged to respond with feelings to the stories of bravery, danger and success.

Although an ENP award for an outstanding contribution by a female officer was made at this ceremony, it seemed clear, both at the time and in subsequent interviews and conversations, that European delegates were rather uneasy at the atmosphere and style created. For students of the history of women in policing, there was a particular pleasure in seeing a lifetime achievement medal given to Felicia Shpritzer, the New York Police Department (NYPD) officer who had mounted a legal challenge at the NYPD's failure to promote women to sergeants' posts in the 1960s and won, thus pioneering the way for later integration. The IAWP had not supported her case at the time (Schulz 1998: 78).

conclusions

By the close of the conference we had sampled twenty-four countries and conducted forty-two interviews involving fifty-six individuals. In comparision, it took me over a year in 1987–8 to make contact with and interview about the same number of women officers in Britain and the USA, with the US interviews taking three weeks of intensive work (Heidensohn 1992). We achieved several targets including interviews with officers from four African countries, four Eastern European and three Far Eastern societies. In short we had a 'thick' sample of a group who are otherwise 'thinly' spread and hard to reach both in geographical access and, in some cases, political. While some interview situations were impromptu, they were all broadly similar and thus produced more readily comparable material than could normally be expected with an international sample.

Added value was gained from the serendipitous circumstances of being able to observe and participate in the conference. For almost a week, a kind of instant village was created in the unlikely setting of the Birmingham Convention Centre, a 'village' populated almost wholly by policewomen whose interactions with each other as well as with us as researchers we could record.

Clearly there are both limitations and some disadvantages to using a conference as a source of research material. Ours was a snowball sample with the addition of some local opportunism. Delegates to an event like this will not be representative of the generality of their profession. They are likely to be older, more experienced and with some prior committment to goals of equality. Some had paid all or part of their own expenses, while others were supported by their own forces. IAWP members constituted most of the former, ENP the latter. Some countries were over-represented in relation to their home numbers: about 20 per cent of the total strength of Icelandic policewomen were in attendance. They outnumbered the delegation from Germany where financial constraints had prevented all but a tiny group coming. Although the proportion of women in German forces is relatively low, the numbers are substantial because of the size of the country.

There were some frustrations: not all interviewees turned up as planned. It was a very tiring process and the team, especially the younger ones, were exhausted by the end. English was the conference language, thus nearly all interviews could be conducted in English (the exceptions included one where an interpreter took part and another where French was used). Arguably this restricted us to a very untypical group of officers, but this would be a limitation for us in any case.

By interviewing at this event we reached female officers from Europe, North America, Africa and Australasia. We did so by spending a relatively modest amount of time and money. We achieved good quality control through preparation and teamwork. As unlooked-for gains we gathered much observational and ethnographic data on the community of female officers. None of them, of course, was policing. Indeed, we were all working while they were training or relaxing. We recorded and observed them as they developed the distinctive international 'sisterhood' of policing by women, a phenomenon already a century old yet still in formation. As 'strangers' we could watch, note and question and use their conference for our own ends.

Reflecting on the issues which I highlighted earlier, there are distinctive aspects to each one. *Access* to the subjects we wished to interview was freely achieved; although the time we had was limited, using a team approach and exploiting the full availability of delegates enabled us to reach our targets in both number and range of contacts. Some subjects did elude us, tantalizingly so, as we saw them in the Conference Centre and its environment. Our surmise about their unwillingness to participate was that they were from forces where some of the problems faced by female officers are at their most acute, but this is supposition. There may have been cultural factors too, since officers from nations where the status of women has improved only recently did volunteer and were often very keen to talk to us.

Relationships with subjects were very good to excellent and, like Reiner (1991), we found ourselves being recommended by interviewees who had enjoyed taking part in, and valued, the project. Some clearly felt that they were contributing to a study which, by recording their experiences and presenting them externally and within an 'objective' academic framework, would bring about change. A few had themselves conducted research in their own forces or in the course of gaining qualifications. Breaking down barriers of suspicion or hostility, as recounted in so much of the literature, was not an issue. Interestingly, one officer who had responded negatively to an earlier request for interview changed her mind at the congress and agreed to talk to us.

It is very likely that many respondents assumed that, while they were well aware that none of us were serving officers, we were in some senses taking their 'standpoint' in our project. From the transcripts it is clear that many, especially from what we have called 'cop' countries of the USA and Britain (see Brown and Heidensohn 2000), took for granted shared values of fairness, feminism and equality. One issue which we had not anticipated and is both a serious and important one concerns the balance of power in the interview relationship. By and large, most discussions of this topic focus on either close rapport between interviewer and subject *or* on the dominance of the former and the relative impotence of subjects (see Oakley 1998 for a review). Although we offered, as I indicated above, a choice to interviewees and some opted for a 'match' with themselves in terms of age, there were one or two occasions where very senior officers saw the more junior members of the team. This raised points about who was in charge, the direction of the interview and its place and time. This is an important matter which is only just being addressed in the feminist literature (Silvestri forthcoming); although some references occur in studies of elite groups (for example Crewe 1974) they do not analyse these aspects which relate to our concerns. Feminists have arguably been less interested in high status women than in women who are vulnerable or victims.

observations

The Birmingham event afforded remarkable and unparalleled observational opportunities. These were, of course, paradoxical because none of the hundreds of delegates was on policing duty – the conference was a training event, so it could be claimed that they were at work, as were those organizers who were police officers. This raises a number of issues about validation and the problems of reliability and validity of material gathered in this setting. Brewer (1990a: 586) discusses the difficulty of RUC officers' being 'truthful' with the fieldworker and whether they hid behind masks. The context he describes here is very different and distinctive: a police station in Belfast before the ceasefire and with a female, Catholic fieldworker. Yet, while access and relationships in Birmingham were at once easy and exceptionally good, queries about validation need to be answered in two senses. First, the interviewees were away, often a very long way, from home. None of the usual checks could be made on the content of what they said. Against these points, it can be argued that the relatively high profile which we as researchers had (discussed above) ensured something of a constraint because of our known range of contacts. Further, several interviews were conducted with groups where pretence or distortion would have been very hard to sustain. Finally, there was no point in making up any information for the interviews. Unlike Brewer's RUC officers who were fearful of serious consequences to themselves, our subjects had no comparable anxieties. (Those who did not participate may have had other fears about the outcome of the experience for them.)

A more complex issue is the way in which the conference became a series of public stages in which delegates performed their roles and how we recorded and interpreted this. We concluded that the links we saw being established or reinforced were genuine. Our privileged positions and our team reporting enabled us to note many exchanges and interactions outside the interview slots. Thus various groups' movements were regularly described to me because I was known to be interested in them. Again, there would have been very little gain from acting out a misleading performance.

Another aspect is how full a picture we could gather from what we saw. We did not follow delegates far off site, on shopping trips or tourist outings, for instance, although we did meet them in their hotels and the local restaurants. More broadly, we did not see them, though some gave us vivid and detailed descriptions, in their own places.

postmodern setting

Many of the international delegates were surprised by the conference venue. They had expected England to offer them tradition and antiques: indeed the event had been advertised in promotional material which stressed proximity to Stratford-upon-Avon and Warwick Castle. The previous congress hosted in Britain was held at Bramshill Police College in a splendid country mansion set in extensive grounds. One delegate aptly described the Conference Centre as a 'postmodern palace'. It is a modern structure which does not defer to any historic links and is notable for the complexities and disjunctures of its design. For our study, what was remarkable was the way its spaces were colonized and used by delegates, transforming it into an instant and ephemeral spectacle. Rock (1993, 1996) has written extensively on architecture and the relationships between social control and spatial structures, but I think that this is a unique account of using space in this way. For our purposes it was indeed serendipitous.

notes

1 The nearest to this report which I can find in criminology are the following:

- George Mair and Tim Newburn (1996) 'Signs of the times: an analysis of the subject matter of papers presented at ASC meetings and British criminology conferences – 1987 to 1995'. Paper presented to the American Society of Criminology Meetings, Chicago, 22 November 1996.
- Stan Cohen's (1995) satirical piece on attending conferences in the *Scottish Journal of Criminal Justice Studies*.
- David Lodge has, of course, satirized the academic conference circuit in *Small World*. But all these are examples of academic not professional or other events.
- Mark Pogrebin and his colleagues at the University of Colorado, Denver, attempted a similar project at an IAWP conference, but did not achieve satisfactory results (Mark Pogrebin, personal communication, 1999).

2 Jenny Brown was a member of the UK group planning the conference and thus had first hand knowledge of the event.
3 This study was funded by an award from the Leverhulme Trust whose support and consideration I most gratefully acknowledge.
4 The other researchers who took part in the study in addition to Jenny Brown and myself were Nikki Batten, Jane Creaton and Marisa Silvestri.
5 Nikki Batten maintained a log of events during the conference on which I have drawn in writing this account.

considering criminology

The turn of the new century found criminologists reflecting on their subject, its roots and future direction, especially with respect to theory. Almost all the end of the 1990s presidents of the American Society of Criminology considered these themes in their addresses to the society's annual conference. Freda Adler was concerned that 'criminology is . . . lagging. How will our theoretical heritage fare?' (Adler 1996: 4), although she was fairly confident that the 'general malaise about the state of criminological theory' (Adler 1996: 6) would pass. She upheld the value of several older approaches to the study of crime. Charles Wellford (1997: 6) advocated a return to 'multi-disciplinary approaches' while also arguing for the rehabilitation of labelling theory and interactionism. Margaret Zalm (1999: 2–5) urged the incorporation of new disciplines and emphasized the need for strategies to enhance the status of criminology in academia.

These authors are continuing a well established practice. Indeed, because criminology is a field of study rather than a discipline, it has to be renewed in this way. What distinguishes the 1990s and 2000s is first the range of the new sources being selected to bring new inspiration or paradigms and second, that there have been a number of studies which have sought to assess *influence* and *impact* in the subject. The aim of this chapter is to review the modern history of our subject, taking account of such work and then to suggest how it can be reinvigorated from new, or reassessed, intellectual sources.

Criminology has always been reviewed and strengthened from outside. The sociology of deviance of the 1960s and 1970s had drawn on a range of theories not previously used by criminologists (Rock 1979; Sumner 1994). The 'new' criminology of the 1970s (Taylor *et al.* 1973) claimed to be a 'fully social theory' of deviance taking neoMarxism as well as interactionism as its revitalizing life forces. Situational crime prevention, while presented as a pragmatic approach to problems, has obvious roots in rational choice theory. Left realism's antecedents are more contested between its proponents and critics (Morgan *et al.* 1994; Young 1994).

For the purposes of this chapter, however, we are less interested in tracing genealogies carefully backwards, even though that may be an important and appropriate task at certain times (Downes and Rock 1988: 12). Our aim is rather, given the alleged and recurring crises in the subject, how best to assess, understand and possibly bring about such changes. In exploring these themes we shall draw particularly on two projects on which we have worked (Rafter and Heidensohn 1995a; Heidensohn with Silvestri 1996).

impact and influence in criminology

The value of what might be called the 'fresh transfusion' model of renewal in criminology does not go unchallenged. Sumner (1994) produced an extended 'obituary' for the sociology of deviance, although he acknowledged its past worth. Stan Cohen (1994) questioned the relevance of left realist approaches to the problems of new democracies and transitional economies and Morrison (1994) in the same volume of essays warned against importing postmodernist perspectives into criminology.

Nevertheless, Braithwaite's (1992) claim probably sums up the views of many contemporary criminologists: 'we need a theoretical revolution in criminology to extricate us from our contemporary nihilism' (Braithwaite 1992: 1). Even if renewal is not achieved through this process, self-reflection and analysis are surely prerequisites for all soundly based academic subjects. The editors of *The Oxford Handbook* do express some in its first edition and caution about developing taxonomies of criminological work in order to better explore underlying assumptions and institutional affiliations . . . we doubt that most contemporary criminology can so easily be classified.

(Morgan *et al*. 1994: 78)

their approach is towards 'a catholicity of theoretical taste' (Morgan *et al*. 1994: 78). One of the two chapters in that volume which does deal solely with the intellectual history and development of the field (Young 1994) has its taxonomy and analysis challenged by the editors in their introduction (Morgan *et al*. 1994: 7–8).

The situation is particularly diagnosed by Nelken (1994) as one in which criminology is isolating itself from the mainstream and failing

to keep up with intellectual developments elsewhere . . . little attention has yet been given to the theoretically daring work which is being done in disciplines such as linguistics, semiotics, cultural studies, social theory or anthropology.

(Nelken 1994: 2)

Those who may not wholly share these anxieties about keeping at the cutting edge of intellectual life might acknowledge that our subject is usually refreshed from outside sources. Rock (1973, 1979) has addressed this topic several times, despite his own cogently expressed view of British criminology that 'despite its nostalgia for the theoretical, it is no longer a discipline besotted with the idea of big ideas' (Rock 1994: 147).

Perhaps it should be surprising that despite the concerns outlined above, consideration of the questions we raised at the beginning of this chapter, namely how to assess, understand and bring about change and influence in our field have begun to be addressed only quite recently. There are, of course, examples of what might be called the 'founding fathers' (*sic*) school (Mannheim 1960) but it is just such analyses which have been challenged in more recent studies by rigorous revisionist historians. Beirne (1988), for example, has argued cogently for a reassessment of the 'legendary status' of Goring's *The English Convict* (TEC) (1913): 'My intention . . . is . . . to take issue on a number of fronts, with the legendary view that TEC's intervention in criminology chiefly represented a definitive refutation of Lombrosianism' (Beirne 1988: 316).

It is possible to identify three broad categories of approach to estimating and analysing impact and influence in criminology:

- measurement indices
- network and process analysis
- historical revisions.

(We make no apologies for these fairly arbitrary categories: we shall be delighted if others criticize and improve on them.)

measurement indices

Several criminologists have undertaken surveys, based on questionnaires and sometimes interviews as well, administered to their colleagues in order to ascertain (among other things) key influences on their intellectual development and current thinking. Marie Andrée Bertrand and colleagues at the Centre for the Study of Comparative Criminology in Montréal surveyed both Canadian criminologists and their writings to assess particularly feminist influences and output (Bertrand 1994). Rock (1988a, 1994) also conducted two pieces of research designed to map out British criminology and identify key influences. Whereas Bertrand (1994: 48) finds some concordance between theoretical influences and research for Canadians, albeit a somewhat complex one, Rock (1994: 141) found that British criminologists were likely to acknowledge fertile impact from interactionism and critical criminology while conducting studies on, for the most part, aspects of the criminal justice system.

The key, and most controversial, contributions to this form of assessment have come from Cohn and Farrington (1990, 1994, 1998) following a pattern set much earlier by Wolfgang *et al.* (1978). Cohn and Farrington's (1994) approach is exemplified in the title of their second article, 'Who are the most influential criminologists in the English-speaking world?' Using citations in four journals they produce rankings of the most often cited criminologists, arguing that citation indices are a valid and reliable measure of influence. Much of their argument is based on the congruence between their ranking measures and other ratings – for example which academic journals are most widely read – and the support given to such work in the discipline of psychology. Their paper provoked strongly worded (and typically effervescent) responses from Mike Levi (1994b, 1995), first in the *British Society of Criminology Newsletter* and then in the correspondence pages of the *British Journal of Criminology*, where Cohn and Farrington (1995) also offer a reply and further justification.

For the purposes of this chapter, the most telling comments from Levi (1995) concern a key term:

> Cohn and Farrington fail to define sufficiently thoughtfully the term influence, which can mean anything from 'commonly used data source' to 'inspiring theoretician'... 'Influence' is also a far fudgier concept than is implied in the Cohn and Farrington treatment of the term, which further assumes that we are aware of what influences us is a highly questionable assumption. Where are Durkheim, Freud, Marx, Weber or for that matter, Leslie Wilkins in the list of the good and the great 'influences'?
>
> (Levi 1995: 138–9)

In their rejoinder, Cohn and Farrington repeat their statement from their original piece that 'we operationally define the most influential criminologists as those who are most cited in the major criminological journals' (Cohn and Farrington 1995: 143).

In the last article from the same team, Cohn and Farrington (1998) reject the more challenging title, 'Who are the most influential criminologists in the English-speaking world?' of their first piece in favour of the modest 'Changes in the most-cited scholars in major international journals . . .'. In comparing two periods (1986–90 and 1991–5) they noted consistency in the rankings of most cited authors in two journals, but not in the other two. They also suggest that *numbers* of citations is not such a good measure of 'one scholar's influence on a large number of other scholars' as *prevalence* of citations. Cohn and Farrington also point out that awareness of such techniques, and publication of analyses such as their own, 'might lead to undesirable changes in citation behaviour' (Cohn and Farrington 1998: 168). This is at least an acknowledgement of the social context and some of the consequent complexities in the real world of scholarship. In Britain, for instance, the Research Assessment Exercises, carried out every four years, are likely to affect publishing patterns for university-based researchers.

Following this series, further variations on this form of analysis have been published, some of which challenge the whole enterprise. Wright (1995, 1996) and his colleagues have produced different rank orders depending on whether text books or journals were scanned. Wright and Sheridan (1997) conclude:

> lists of the most-cited scholars and works are no more representative of a discipline or a speciality than the publications that researchers choose to analyze. As an example, one reason that Cohn and Farrington typically find so many quantitative researchers among their most-cited criminologists is that they analyze mostly quantitative journals.
>
> (Wright and Sheridan 1997: 55)

In fact, in their latest work, Cohn and Farrington (1998: 156), taking four international journals, observed that 'the most-cited works of the most-cited scholars in the later period were more concerned with criminological theories'. This suggests possible evidence of renewal or revival (Hirschi and Braithwaite are among those listed) but unfortunately, Cohn and Farrington (1998) do not explore the production of criminological knowledge or the sociology of influence any further than this.

Wright does engage with these questions, both by pointing out the varied outcomes possible by selecting from different sources and especially, in his joint paper on women and crime, by proposing that this study might aid scholars:

> extensive citation helps the career advancement of academics. Scholars . . . can receive a crucial boost by appearing on a list of most-cited scholars . . . We hope that our study will help advance the careers of notable woman scholars and/or women and crime researchers.
>
> (Wright and Sheridan 1997: 56)

This study neatly points up an irony of such work, and one that these analyses can highlight, but not explore. The authors deliberately chose publications on women and crime and by women scholars *because* they are omitted from, or marginalized in, mainstream work. They remark that their most cited scholars do not feature in the Cohn and Farrington series. Feminist criminologists have raised the question of their impact over a long period (see for example Heidensohn 1987; Gelsthorpe and Morris 1988, 1990) and noted some improvement and recognition (Heidensohn 1996; Gelsthorpe 1997). Citation studies can illustrate the problem, but cannot offer solutions.

There is some, if somewhat limited, value in all the approaches involving numbers to estimating influence, although Levi (1995) is surely right in insisting that citation counts measure just that and not the more complex and subjective matter of influence. He considers the Cohn and Farrington technique to be pointless and possibly damaging. We would suggest that such measures can be useful and that at least a debate has been opened up and, incidentally, recipe guides as to how to be frequently quoted offered.

network and process analysis

Some of the authors cited above as measuring influence have also tried to describe networks of influence. Rock (1994) has, using survey material on about 100 British criminologists, outlined their generational, educational and academic links. He portrays this social world as a 'lattice-work' and urges

> those who would understand the history and significance of British criminology ... [to] recognize criminology as a structure of power and politics, searching for the gatekeepers, the institutions, and the men and women who have the influence to determine who and what shall thrive in the discipline.
>
> (Rock 1994: 125–6)

He depicts – as he did in an earlier article (Rock 1988a) a subject in which a 'fortunate generation' of middle-aged academics dominate from posts they achieved in the 1960s and 1970s. Their intellectual formation was through the 'Big Bang' of the 'new theories' of the 1960s and although their research is now predominantly on law enforcement, their teaching is still focused on theory. There is a 'nostalgia for the theoretical' but feminism has not spread among this 'masculine' discipline (Rock 1994: 146–7).

Rock recounts in some detail the situation of academic production in Britain as it has particularly affected criminology, noting some key networks and generational links. The picture he paints here is very different from that sketched by Stan Cohen (1971) in a now classic essay on the state of British criminology, revised a decade after it first appeared (Cohen 1981). Cohen reviews more institutional history than Rock does and describes a criminological establishment characterized by 'pragmatism, the interdisciplinary conception, correctionalism and positivism' (Cohen 1981: 222) which remained unmoved by a decade's ferment of new ideas. He did find responses to the new deviancy in sociology, but the world he depicts does not match very well with Rock's (Rock does not cite Cohen's paper here) not least because he did not include the same type of material but gives his own historical account.

However, in a later collection Rock and Holdaway (1998) took a different and very fruitful approach to significant aspects of the questions we are raising in this chapter. The editors asked

> a number of criminologists who have already made their mark ... to stand back and reflect upon the ideas that underpin their work ... to describe their more theoretical pre-occupations, examine what bearing they have had upon their work ... [to] lay bare the more or less tacit theorising that ... informs current criminology.
>
> (Rock and Holdaway 1998: 11–12)

Eight criminologists who were mainly, but not all, based in Britain responded with a range of accounts which are very illuminating. (Frances Heidensohn is one of the authors.) Rock and Holdaway outline some of the history of the development of criminology in Britain, recalling Rock's earlier research on the 'fortunate generation' and on this occasion, citing Cohen. In introducing their authors, Rock and Holdaway (1998: 11) note the intertwining of 'theorizing ... with the subjective and the biographical'. The eight authors catalogue many influences and turning points, epiphanies and digressions which cannot easily be summed up into any general findings. The editors do not try to do this, although they pick out some common features of careers such as political commitments. What they do end by asserting is 'theory is inevitable and integral'.

The criminologists in *Thinking about Criminology* do enable us to suggest some ways in which patterns of inspiration and renewal in our field can be examined. For example, questions of the sociology of knowledge and its production in universities and other research bodies is of great importance as is the direction of development in teaching. Rock's 'fortunate generation' were sponsored by the expansion of British higher education. At a quite different level, the eight authors acknowledge stimulus from a much wider universe than the one that the citation studies map. Finally, while this is not made explicit in the collection, the networks stressed by Rock are very evident: most obviously in the responding authors, but also in many of their histories of overlap, common concerns and approaches. Striking, too, are the *omissions* (although their work is cited) none of the left realists, nor 'idealists' from Britain (although Nils Christie is here). Their absence is surely also an indication of the existence of what Rock calls a lattice.

Bertrand's (1994) Canadian study explored some parallel network themes although it does not address issues about knowledge production. (Rock himself does touch on these in Canada in his comparative account of the growth of the victim movement there (1987).)

Again there are many lessons to learn from these studies. Both Rock and Cohen assess influence subjectively: whom or what is claimed to be an influence is counted as such although Cohen records observations of a situation, that of established criminology in Britain, which he sought to challenge and change and then to map later stages of that process while Rock monitors responses another decade further on. Each assumes certain definitions of influence and impact: Cohen uses evidence of *change*, especially the acceptance of once radical ideas, whereas Rock's measure is multidimensional and allows for continuity as well as change. Peter Young (1992) has, of course, in turn challenged Cohen's account of criminology insisting on the existence of 'deeper structures' of a utopian kind which underpin values and concerns (Young 1992: 429–30). Young also makes another salient point about receptivity to new ideas: 'it is only if a claim to knowledge is framed in terms of a recognizable criminological tradition that it is allowed, as it were, into the kirk' (Young 1992: 426).

historical revisions

All the above accounts of reported influences in criminology have a historical base and also include some analysis of the structures, demography, cultures and economy of the modes of academic production of criminology in Britain. The fullest, most detailed analyses yet produced to contribute to our understanding of influence in criminology have come from revisionist histories of intellectual thought, above all in the work of Garland (1985, 1988, 1992, 1994) and also of Beirne (1988, 1993). These are complex versions and treat of many aspects, but one of the key issues which Garland addresses in charting the development of criminology is *power*, power that is, both within the discipline and in the changing and diverse institutional settings in which it is practised. While Foucault (1977) had earlier presented insights related to this, Garland (1992) points out that Foucault does not allow in his analysis for more than one genealogy in its history. For Foucault, 'power-knowledge' is the key (and the sole) axis of influence; Garland (1992: 413) stresses that 'criminology's pattern of borrowing from its constituent disciplines has changed over time. Criminology has been an eclectic, interdisciplinary endeavour virtually from its beginnings'. One of the most interesting points to emerge from Garland's work is his questioning of the 'Big Bang' model of impact espoused both by the 'new' theorists of the 1960s and 1970s and by later accounts such as those of Cohen and Rock (Garland 1994: 60–1).

lessons on impact

In attempting to assess the impact of new ideas on criminology we suggest that several key concepts can be derived from other writers' attempts to deal with this question. First, the question is obviously an important one and one that some of the most thoughtful criminologists have engaged in and are increasingly doing so. Second, no consensus exists on measures; this, as with criminology itself in many versions, is a contested topic. Third, it is critical to have as full a version, sociologically speaking, as possible, in terms of the sites, forms and so on of the production of knowledge. Further, it is clear that a crucial by-product of this is the publishing of 'canonical' accounts. Thus, most modern versions of modern criminology and its antecedents are written by participants in the 'Big Bang'. Finally two models of recent patterns of impact can be discerned: the 'Big Bang' view of the changes wrought by the explosions of modern deviancy theory (Cohen and Rock) and the contrasting view taken by Garland (and Beirne) that criminology does not develop in this way, is much more contingent and complex, what might be character-ized as the 'slow burn' model. (Although the Holdaway and Rock (1998) volume seems to support the latter version in the indi-vidual accounts as they are presented, while their framework is perhaps that of the 'Big Bang'.) We shall now review our own attempts to assess the impact of feminism on criminology within these frameworks. It is worth noting that most of the authors quoted so far refer specifically to feminism and its impact, but while according ritual acknowledgement, they either can not find real signs of influence (Rock 1994) or fail to produce an appropriate analysis (Nelken 1994). Holdaway and Rock (1998) do include two feminist authors. Bertrand (1994), whose aim was to document changes in feminist impact, is one exception and so is an interesting paper by South (1996).

South (1996) in reviewing the state of 'late-modern criminology' takes the feminist critique of and dialogue with the subject as a central theme. He observes that Smart's (1990) objections to criminology are not well sustained, but at the same time notes that criminology has continued to be revitalized by feminist theories, among others.

We sought to assess the impact of feminism for two projects. One involved the revision of *Women and Crime* which Heidensohn had published in 1985. In order to provide material for the second edition we needed to assess how much the field of criminology had altered during the previous decade; among the questions we had to consider was the effect of feminism. To ascertain this we employed aspects of all three approaches outlined above. Marisa Silvestri searched databases and citation indices for articles and books published since 1985 on the topics of women and crime, gender and crime, feminist perspectives and so on (Heidensohn with Silvestri 1996).

Some two hundred items were categorized under eight headings according to their main subject content:

1 Historical
2 Juvenile
3 Race/ethnic
4 Judicial processing
5 Prison
6 Specific crimes
7 Crime causation
8 Feminist discourse/theory.

By far the largest grouping was specific crimes with articles on prostitution and drugs and drugs-related offences predominating, although prisons and crime causation both registered twenty-five items and judicial processing twenty-three. We did not try to assess the 'feminist stance' of those studies as Bertrand *et al.* (1992) did. Instead, we concluded that four main features characterized them, and indeed much other recent criminology. These were that feminism has a high *recognition* factor in most work, with authors acknowledging, and sometimes writing to, an altered script and with varied commitment to using such perspectives. Obviously, we also noted the *expansion* in work on women and crime, much of which is quite clearly inspired by questions raised by some feminist writers. Thus, for example, we identified fifteen gender-bias studies relating to judicial processes published between 1986 and 1993 whereas Heidensohn had located only four of these for the first edition of *Women and Crime* (Heidensohn 1985).

Two further trends which we observed in this considerable body of work and which are perhaps more explicitly related to the aims of feminist scholars are the *engendering* of the criminological *agenda* and the *deconstruction* of many taken-for-granted categories. The latter is an epistemological approach neither exclusive nor original to feminism, but one that feminists have so far taken further than others (Nelken 1994). By engendering the agenda we mean that gender issues and especially the gendered nature of a considerable amount of crime has been acknowledged – domestic violence, for instance. 'Deconstruction' is the process of rethinking the meaning and categorization of terms and topics so that none can be assumed to have substance. Thus the very terms 'women' and 'crime' have been challenged and presented as problematic.

The main purpose of this work was not to estimate the impact of feminism in criminology but to analyse and assess recent research on women and crime and to decide what had affected it and in what directions it was moving. Attempting to estimate feminism's impact on this body of knowledge was only one of the tasks.

The second project we are considering here was different in emphasis: it involved the preparatory work for another study (Rafter and Heidensohn 1995a). The purpose of this work was quite explicitly to assess the impact feminism has had on criminology in a number of countries. It developed as the result of a major conference on women and law and social control held in Canada in 1991 and from a series of meetings at later international conferences, including meetings of the American Society of Criminology and the 1993 British Criminology Conference.

Through these meetings and other contacts, we invited a number of scholars to contribute their own evaluations of feminism's encounter with criminology in their own country. One study reports on Bertrand's (1995) experiences in three northern European countries. (The nations covered are Australia, South Africa, Britain, Italy, Poland, Germany, Denmark, Finland, Canada and the USA. We did try to commission chapters from other parts of Europe and especially from the South, but were not successful.)

Many points of interest arise when comparing the different approaches of our authors. Among the most significant for the purposes of this chapter are those concerning

- definitions
- local institutions and structures
- common measures of impact.

definitions

The authors define, and redefine, feminism, impact and criminology in various ways. One striking feature is the recent, restricted range of criminology reported from several countries (for example Australia and Poland) and its particular history. Tamar Pitch at first responded to our request for a chapter on Italy by saying that she 'couldn't do it' and then going on to explain that feminism has been a powerful and effective movement in Italy, but that what has been achieved is the 'reframing' of social problems and the reshaping of social policies rather than influencing crimino-logy. So Pitch (1995) redirects the question to explore this area and to observe that Italian criminology is still caught in the twin grips of 'jurisprudence' and 'clinical criminology' and that critical criminology had only a limited and brief role in Italian crimino-logy. Hansson (1995), too, devotes space in her chapter to chart-ing the distinctive development of criminology in South Africa and its particular local 'nationalist' and 'fundamentalist' forms and the later appearance of 'progressive-realist' criminology which has proved a relatively sympathetic home to some aspects of feminism.

local institutions and structures

Several of our contributors point to the importance of particular local political situations in handling the theme of the book. Alder (1995) insists that the colonial history of Australia and the role of the state in welfare has meant that feminists there have not needed to avoid state power or state bureaucracies. Indeed, she argues that there is a form of 'femocracy' there which has enabled feminists to have limited but important influence in criminal justice policies. The rise and fall of communism is central to Platek's (1995) analysis of the situation in Poland both in relation to the position of women there and to changes in criminology. She sees the post-communist changes as having radicalized Polish women.

We asked our contributors to comment on the conditions of academic knowledge production in their respective countries, especially as it affected criminology. The two chapters by Canadian scholars focus exclusively on these. Bertrand (1995) compares university criminology in Europe very unfavourably with its counterparts in North America. Chunn and Menzies (1995) use data from their survey of Anglophone Canadian criminologists to outline the career patterns of criminology postgraduates and in particular the differing experience of women and men. In writing about Britain Heidensohn (1995) pointed to the import-ance of the range of sites of production outside the academy here and the alternative modes of production of criminology among the numerous pressure, lobby and research groups in the field.

common measures of impact

Most authors, although the project involved essentially a self-assessment of the impact question, attempted to use a range of simple measures to check the impact of feminism. Thus the growth in the numbers studying was mentioned (Chunn and Menzies 1995) as well as increases in those holding academic posts in the USA (Rafter and Heidensohn 1995a) numbers (and quality) of academic outputs (Hansson 1995; Heidensohn 1995).

While the contributors to *International Feminist Perspectives in Criminology* employ common devices to estimate their subject's effectiveness, it is clear that in practice impact – or the lack of it – is being judged in a largely subjective way. Several contributors emphasized the second half of our question, which asked about the effect on criminal justice policy and the criminal justice system of feminist perspectives. While North American authors were less likely to stress this, Klein (1995) began her piece from this angle, highlighting the huge moral panic about crime in the USA and the radical approach she proposes to counter this. In the reports on Australia, South Africa, Italy and Britain developments in the treatment of victims and of crimes against women – what Hansson (1995) calls 'patriarchal violence' – are highlighted as consequences of feminism. Platek (1995) points out, on the other hand, as evidence of Poland's singularity, that recognition of victims and their needs there has *not* included the same focus on women as in North America. Bertrand (1995) confesses herself perplexed that in Denmark, Germany, Norway and Finland – liberal states with sophisticated feminist movements – there has been so little take up or integration of these approaches in criminology.

When preparing our introduction to *International Feminist Perspectives in Criminology* (1995a), Nicky Rafter and Frances Heidensohn did not attempt a final measure of impact on criminology in each country. We found that each account was so diverse that this was not feasible. It is, however, worth commenting that the greatest confidence and optimism is shown by Alder (1995) and Hansson (1995), who write about situations (in Australia and South Africa) where, for various historical reasons, no strongly institutionalized establishment of criminology exists. In Australia, Alder (1995) argues, criminology is a small enterprise and much research work is conducted outside universities in sites where feminists employed in state bureaucracies can determine its agenda. 'Progressive realist' criminology is the rising form in South Africa, argues Hansson (1995) and, conceived in the period of struggle against apartheid, it remains open, with 'pliable' edges to feminism.

However, all the chapters on North America and Europe, from countries where criminology has an older, stronger base, are more sceptical. Optimism mostly derives from experience which shows that applying feminist perspectives does bring about change. What changes, however, is more likely to be an aspect of the criminal justice system, such as police handling of rape victims or incidents of domestic violence. Or the media may present issues in a new framework: witness the handling of cases of violence and abuse in British television 'soaps' such as *Brookside* and *EastEnders* and the sophisticated use of the media by campaigners on behalf of imprisoned women. As Pitch (1995) reports from Italy, feminist activists may bypass criminology and criminal justice altogether in order to achieve progress on an issue such as Mafia terrorism or heroin trafficking by expressing their concerns as private citizens who have been harmed.

The difference between these accounts and those of the rest of our authors lies in a core issue. It is not of enormous significance whether or not feminism influences criminology in these countries because criminology is not very significant. In contrast in the USA, Canada, Britain and in some parts of Scandinavia, there are institutional forms of criminology, indeed one could be bolder (reckless?) and say that these are the sources from whence most key criminological ideas flow. That is why feminists have to a degree sought to influence criminological thought in those places and are concerned at their so far limited impact.

That their impact is so far modest is their own sober assessment. Yet that statement takes us back to our starting point. How should we assess influence in criminology? Can we propose a model or models of patterns of influence? We suggested above three central themes which we derived from our reading of earlier approaches to questions of influence. We noted two conceptions of how influence works: 'Big Bang' versus 'Slow Burn' and also how vital it was to have proponents of new ideas as evangelists of the canon when it comes to be written. Some feminists have seen their ideas as equal to a big bang, presenting a major challenge to the field, yet it is clear that they have impact, where they do, only through a burn that is so slow and gradual it can best be described as a smoulder.

What our perusal of earlier (and largely non-feminist) work on influences in criminology also showed was the importance of understanding the target to be influenced – the criminological establishment – and its history, sociology and politics. Yet it does not take a very sophisticated analysis to demonstrate that established criminology is not generally penetrated or overthrown. Rather the successful examples of change and renewal come from finding *new sites* and *new spaces*. Thus Cohen's (1981) 'footprints in the sand' did not lead directly into the Home Office or the Cambridge Institute of Criminology, but rather into the expanding departments of sociology in the polytechnics and newer universities of the 1960s and 1970s (as Rock 1988a indeed demonstrates).

In 1999, Leon Radzinowicz, last of the three Europeans who founded and formed British criminology, published his memoirs, the summation of a very long and distinguished career in the subject. Among its many aspects, this book includes Radzinowicz's (1999: 229) version of the setting up of the National Deviancy conference in 'opposition' to the establishment in the form of the Cambridge Institute of Criminology. It may be that this version of the history of criminological development in Britain (the memoirs cover much else as well) will come to be included in the canon. Certainly, it provides a new genealogy for our subject's origins here (Sparks 1999).

Indeed, as Heidensohn (1995) tried to show in her own contribution to *International Feminist Perspectives in Criminology* many younger criminologists have sought new sites and spaces outside the academy. Partly this has been the inevitable result of the limited expansion of academic posts in the late twentieth century (Rock 1994) and also of the low levels of mobility of the 'fortunate generation'. Instead of taking posts in universities they have moved into criminal justice professions, pressure groups and also into commercially sponsored work. Pitch (1995) makes a similar point about Italy.

Much of the 'resistance' to innovation in the late 1990s reflected the relative lack of such new opportunities, in Britain at least, since the early 1980s. This situation is about to change and it is instructive to speculate on what will happen when a generation (to which one of us belongs) reared on Becker and Matza retires.

A glance at the material assembled by Rock (1994) and Chunn and Menzies (1995) suggests that success may come by succession and that perhaps when the younger of us comes to write her version of the canon, she will be able to rewrite the history of influences.

(We have for the purposes of this chapter not considered the question of the nature and quality of the ideas whose impact we are measuring. The history of criminology, as that of other areas of social science, is full of examples of simple, sometimes almost trivial, concepts which have profoundly affected their field. Often, as commentators tirelessly point out, the ideas are not new at all but are merely repackaged or reformulated. We would be prepared to argue that feminist approaches have much to offer criminology, especially if they are more broadly interpreted, but that is a theme outside the scope of this chapter.)

There is in short, no recipe for creating an impact in criminology. Peter Young (1992) has suggested that novel perspectives require an affinity with established ones in order to achieve acceptance while Stan Cohen (1981) argues that it was the force of the radical challenge which helped it to succeed. We would stress from our own work on two related projects that it is through basic social science analysis that we can, as so often, understand this criminological dilemma. It is not, on the whole, the power of ideas which makes them fly. Ideas will have wings when political, historical and social situations are propitious. For them to launch effective missiles (to stretch a metaphor to snapping point) requires local, if not global, conflict and a major production industry in support.

Criminology may be in crisis once more. It may need renewal from fresh sources, which (paradoxically) it seems unable to draw on, although we note South's (1996) confidence on this point. Yet the crisis is perhaps due to a generation (Rock's 'fortunate generation') holding on to place and position while pioneers from younger generations have, even if they have found their place, as yet little space of their own to express themselves in.

If we are right about generation, and perhaps gender, they need only wait.

is the personal political or the political personal?

The most dramatic change in the political scene in the modern era is surely the shift in the relationships between the political and the personal. When Raisa Gorbachev, wife of the former Soviet leader Mikhail Gorbachev, died in the autumn of 1999, her obituaries remarked that she was the first woman in such a position to become a public figure. The spouses of previous Soviet leaders had been largely unknown and invisible. Not only had Raisa become recognized (and at times reviled), but also her role and position had themselves become *politicized*. In other words, private matters – family life, intimate relationships, even dress – were the subject of much comment and speculation.

Both the USA and Britain saw a series of highly publicized events at the very end of the 1990s which illustrated this. In the USA, the Starr Report produced the most detailed and intimate account of President Clinton's relationship with a White House intern, Monica Lewinsky, and this became the basis for an attempt to impeach the president. In Britain, both in the run-up to the 1997 general election and afterwards, the private actions of ministers came under a great deal of scrutiny, with some considerable effect on the outcome of the election as well as on the careers of individual ministers.

While these are very real developments, often attributed to the changed nature of modern journalism and shifts in technology and ownership, there have been other, more profound movements occurring as well, which influenced the trend to 'cult of personality' outlined above, as well as altering the agenda of modern politics. These observations have salience because, I contend, the twenty-first century sees us at a key historical point, not only in terms of dates in the western calendar, but also in questions about the boundaries of politics and their relevance to crime and justice issues. These are of importance to society and its citizens, and also to academic criminology. Defining the concept of 'crime' is not only an exercise for students, but also the substance of debates about issues such as drug use, pornography, parenting and prostitution.

In this final chapter I want to draw together the variations on this theme set out earlier and make some proposals about twenty-first century directions. From the accounts in Chapters 2 and 4 it is clear that the pioneers of first wave feminism succeeded in bringing about a major translation of their own *private concerns* into *public causes*. Frustration with domestic life or the lack of career opportunities was transformed into campaigns to improve the lot of groups of women and the quality of social life and focused, especially in the USA and Britain, on winning the vote. Although political enfranchisement became a major goal in itself, and it is arguable that the movements and their activists became exhausted after achieving it, there is plenty of evidence of another agenda.

One of the main threads linking these pioneers – and sometimes breaking their links – was their recognition of the importance of *social control* to their cause. Indeed many first became engaged in control causes – such as temperance, moral rescue and animal welfare – *before* they joined suffrage groups. Not only did some of them promote the role of policewomen, but also they worked on altering the scope and shape of the politics of social control. It is possible to summarize the underlying interests as the *policing of private behaviour which had public consequences*. Thus soliciting and enticement, excessive drinking, any waywardness by children or young women all became targets. This represented a real redrawing of frontiers and disputes about territory. In addition, many of these pioneers were influential in the wider policy programme of the early twentieth century which involved the *socialization of private behaviour which had social consequences*. There is a huge literature on the history of social welfare which records and analyses policies designed to improve the maternal skills of working-class women (Lewis 1980) and to 'domesticate' the treatment of fallen women (Mahood 1990) and of young delinquents (Appier 1998). This seismic shift which moved much 'deviant' behaviour into the tutelage of the informal and voluntary sphere was not solely the work of women. They did, however, play major roles and were resourceful in setting up new schemes when they lost territory.

In Chapter 3 I considered the contributions that women pro-testors have made to the history of political violence. This is an under-reported and under-recorded area: accounts tend to be of the personal rather than a political kind. Yet such actions do need to find their place in a review of new forms of politics. For instance, the likely effects of growing legitimate participation by women in the armed forces and in contact sports (a woman boxer fought – and won – a match against a male opponent in Seattle as I was writing this in October 1999). For women and for small children, close personal relationships remain the most likely setting where harm and abuse will occur. A 'new' politics would have to take on board the consequences of removing barriers here.

Late twentieth century feminists took a different path from their forebears in relation to defining boundaries. They too focused on social control as a core issue, but this has tended to be some-what masked in the way it has been presented. Domestic violence and abuse became *the* major concern for second wave feminists; their campaigns focused (and continue to do so) on the publiciz-ing of behaviour still deemed 'private', and hence not criminal. Much effort has gone into ensuring that it will be treated as criminal and hence the *policing of private behaviour with personal consequences*. Also, and very importantly, a great deal of endeavour has been expended on ensuring the *socialization of those private consequences* through the setting up of refuges, advocacy and research.

It would be far too optimistic to assert that we can face the twenty-first century with the concerns of nineteenth and twen-tieth century feminists assuaged and their battles won. There are still all too many gross examples of, for instance, prominent sportsmen whose violence towards their partners is widely publi-cized, yet goes unpunished and even condoned. Yet there have been some real changes and the new century will see more.

This must lead to the consideration at least of further changes in the scope and shape of policies in the new era. For instance, returning to the framework which I outlined above, we may well see *the socialization of private behaviour with personal consequences*: indeed, 'parenting' classes might be seen as a harbinger of this as could training programmes for violent and abusing men. Such approaches do raise major questions about private lives and public safety and will certainly have to be addressed because they have profound consequences for society and its forms of control.

In Chapters 5 and 6 of this volume I have tried to address, in relation to the main themes of politics, policy and law and order, what I have come to think of as the post-seminar paper problems. It is a common experience for an academic to give a paper which covers the kinds of subjects included here, often moving in the closing section to relate one's topic to wider themes; among the queries then raised are often questions about how another scholar in an associated area can solve problems in their own research, either in its execution, or in achieving impact and influence with it. There are often implicit assumptions in such enquiries that there exists somewhere a compendium of advice and information which will provide solutions to these dilemmas, or that there are experts or achievers who have done so who will not share their knowledge but can be observed and imitated. This section therefore should respond to some of those questioners and while not providing recipes or manuals, show at least how engagement with research which can make a difference might be approached.

In a sense 'making a difference' to policy and politics is the subtext of this work. This has to be an aspiration for anyone interested in this subject: as Rock (1994) has put it, criminology is 'a structure of power and politics'. While all social sciences share these characteristics to some extent, criminology has its subject matter defined by and in the political processes of nation-states (and sometimes their subdivisions). Even those branches of the subject which draw on radical or critical roots place themselves and their critique in relation to the state. Most of us have begun criminological research either from a wish to affect our own subject, its theories and paradigms, or to change policies which relate to the area, or sometimes both. As I suggested above, there have been periods of disengagement from the improvement or administration of criminal justice. Sometimes distrust or scepticism over particular institutions is manifest: Smart (1989), for example, has questioned whether women can ever achieve justice through a legal system so imbued with particular constructions of the feminine.

While cautious, I am more optimistic and do believe not only in the possibilities of change, but also that these have to be worked on and for and not necessarily via the most obvious paths. I have more knowledge and experience now than when I first wrote about such matters, but that has made me somewhat less sure about the ways of gaining wished-for outcomes. Ours is a reflective and reflexive age and, as suggested in Chapter 6, criminology has been the focus of several research studies which have sought to tease out, through the medium of intellectual autobiography, the complex of the personal and the political in a series of careers. Inevitably, the question of making wider impact arose in the examples used there.

I was one of those subjects (in Holdaway and Rock 1998); I have also responded in the late 1990s to a number of other requests for versions of my own history to be used for instructive purposes (Heidensohn 1997a; Eaton 2000). In an interesting Hawthorne effect, taking part in such projects has led me to change some of my practice, at least as far as this book is concerned. One of my interviewers (not one of those cited above) claimed not to be able to find the answers to certain kinds of questions, especially what she termed 'working out' in what she read. The readers could join up and apply what they saw better for themselves than any author could. In an individualistic, fast-paced age, I think that this view has validity and have in consequence presented here pieces, each of which is distinct in its form and content, but links to the others, and I trust to current and future concerns and agendas. The central figures must then be the readers who will interrogate my text, agree or disagree, arrange and rearrange it to suit them. This I take to be the new reflexivity and the path into future ways of making a difference.

bibliography

Acker, J., Barry, K. and Esseveld, J. (1991) Objectivity and truth: problems in doing feminist research, in M.M. Fonow and J.A. Cook (eds) *Beyond Methodology: Feminist Scholarship as Lived Research*. Bloomington, IN: Indiana University Press.

Adler, F. (1975) *Sisters in Crime*. New York, NY: McGraw-Hill.

Adler, F. (1996) Our American Society of Criminology, the world and the state of the art, *Criminology*, 34(1): 1–9.

Alder, C. (1995) Feminist criminology in Australia, in N. Rafter and F.M. Heidensohn (eds) *International Feminist Perspectives in Criminology: Engendering a Discipline*. Buckingham: Open University Press.

Alder, C.M. and Baker, J. (1997) Maternal filicide: more than one story to be told, *Women and Criminal Justice*, 9(2): 15–39.

Allen, H. (1986) *Justice Unbalanced*. Milton Keynes: Open University Press.

Allen, M. (1925) *The Pioneer Policewoman*. London: Chatto and Windus.

Appier, J. (1998) *The Sexual Politics of Law Enforcement and the LAPD*. Philadelphia, PA: Temple University Press.

Baird Committee (1921) *Committee on the Employment of Women on Police Duties*. Minutes of Evidence, Cmd 1133. London: HMSO.

Banks, O. (1981) *Faces of Feminism*. Oxford: Martin Robertson.

Bayley, D. (1985) *Patterns of Policing*. New Brunswick, NJ: Rutgers University Press.

Beaujon, C.M. (1911) *Die Mitarbeit der Frau bei der Polizei*. University of Utrecht, The Hague.

Beck, U. (1992) *The Risk Society*. London: Sage.

Becker, J. (1977) *Hitler's Children*. London: Michael Joseph.

Beirne, P. (1988) Heredity versus environment, *British Journal of Criminology*, 28(3): 315–39.

Beirne, P. (1993) *Inventing Criminology: The Rise of 'Homo Criminalis'.* Albany, NY: State University of New York Press.

Bertrand, M.A. (1994) 1893–1993: from La Donna Delinquente to a postmodern deconstruction of the 'Woman Question' in social control theory, *Journal of Human Justice,* 5(2): 43–57.

Bertrand, M.A. (1995) The place and status of feminist criminology in Germany, Denmark and Finland, in N. Rafter and F.M. Heidensohn (eds) *International Feminists Perspectives in Criminology: Engendering a Discipline.* Buckingham: Open University Press.

Bertrand, M.A., Daly, K. and Klein, D. (eds) (1992) *Proceedings of the International Feminist Conference on Women, Law and Social Control.* Mt Gabriel, Québec.

Beveridge, W. (1942) *Social Insurance and Allied Services,* Cmd 6404. London: HMSO.

Blair, K.J. (1980) *The Clubwoman as Feminist.* New York, NY: Holmes & Meier.

Bland, L. (1992) Feminist vigilantes of late Victorian England, in C. Smart (ed.) *Regulating Womanhood.* London: Routledge.

Bolt, C. (1993) *The Women's Movements in the US and Britain from the 1790s to the 1920s.* Hemel Hempstead: Harvester Wheatsheaf.

Bottoms, A. and Wiles, P. (1992) Explanations of crime and place, in D. Evans, N.R. Fyfe and D.T. Herbert (eds) *Crime, Policing and Place.* London: Routledge.

Bottoms, A. and Wiles, P. (1995) Crime and insecurity in the city, in C. Fijuant, J. Goethals, T. Peters and L. Walgrave (eds) *Changes in Society, Crime and Criminal Justice in Europe.* The Hague: Kluwer.

Braithwaite, J. (1992) Reducing the crime problem: a not so dismal criminology, *Australian and New Zealand Journal of Criminology,* 25.

Brewer, J. (1990a) Sensitivity as a problem in field research, *American Behavioral Scientist,* 33(5): 578–93.

Brewer, J. (1990b) *Inside the RUC: Routine Policing in a Divided Society.* Oxford: Clarendon Press.

Brewer, J. (1991) Hercules, Hippolyte and the Amazons – or policewomen in the RUC, *British Journal of Sociology,* 42(2): 231–47.

Broido, V. (1977) *Apostles into Terrorists.* London: Maurice Temple Smith.

Brooks, B. (1993) A weakness for strong subjects: the women's movement and sexuality, *New Zealand Journal of History,* 27: 140.

Brown, J. (1997) Women in policing: a comparative research perspective, *International Journal of the Sociology of Law,* 25: 1–19.

Brown, J. and Campbell, E.A. (1991) Less than equal, *Policing,* 7: 324–33.

Brown, J. and Heidensohn, F. (2000) *Gender and Policing.* London: Macmillan.

Brown, J., Campbell, E.A. and Fife Schaw, C. (1995) Adverse impacts experienced by police officers following exposure to sex discrimination and sexual harassment, *Stress Medicine,* 11: 221–8.

Browne, A. (1987) *When Battered Women Kill*. London: Collier Macmillan.
Burney, E. (1990) *Putting Street Crime in its Place*. London: Centre for Inner City Studies, Goldsmiths College, University of London.
Cain, M. (ed.) (1990) *Growing up Good*. London: Sage.
Campbell, A. (1981) *Girl Delinquents*. Oxford: Blackwell.
Campbell, A. (1984) *The Girls in the Gang*. Oxford: Blackwell.
Campbell, B. (1993) *Goliath*. London: Methuen.
Carlen, P. (1983) *Women's Imprisonment*. London: Routledge and Kegan Paul.
Carlen, P. (1988) *Women, Crime and Poverty*. Milton Keynes: Open University Press.
Carrier, J. (1988) *The Campaign for the Employment of Women as Police Officers*. Aldershot: Avebury.
Chan, J.B.L. (1997) *Changing Police Culture: Policing in a Multicultural Society*. Cambridge: Cambridge University Press.
Chunn, D.E. and Menzies, R. (1995) Canadian criminology and the 'Woman Question', in N. Rafter and F.M. Heidensohn (eds) *International Feminist Perspectives in Criminology: Engendering a Discipline*. Buckingham: Open University Press.
Coffey, S., Brown, J.M. and Savage, P. (1992) Policewomen's career aspirations: some reflections on the roles and capabilities of British women officers, *Police Studies*, 15: 13–19.
Cohen, S. (ed.) (1971) *Images of Deviance*. Harmondsworth: Penguin.
Cohen, S. (1981) Footprints in the sand: a further report on criminology and the sociology of deviance in Britain, in M. Fitzgerald, G. McLennan and J. Pawson (eds) *Crime and Society: Readings in History and Theory*. London: Routledge and Kegan Paul and Milton Keynes: Open University Press.
Cohen, S. (1994) Social control and the politics of reconstruction, in D. Nelken (ed.) *The Futures of Criminology*. London: Sage.
Cohen, S. (1995) Conference life: the rough guide, *Scottish Journal of Criminal Justice Studies*, 1 (June): 33–59.
Cohn, E.G. and Farrington, D.P. (1990) Differences between British and American criminology: an analysis of citations, *British Journal of Criminology*, 30(4): 467–82.
Cohn, E.G. and Farrington, D.P. (1994) Who are the most influential criminologists in the English-speaking world, *British Journal of Criminology*, 34(2): 204–25.
Cohn, E.G. and Farrington, D.P. (1995) The validity of citations as a measure of influence in criminology, *British Journal of Criminology*, 35(1): 143–5.
Cohn, E.G. and Farrington, D.P. (1998) Changes in the most-cited scholars in major international journals between 1989–90 and 1991–95, *British Journal of Criminology*, 38(1): 156–70.

Corrigan, P. (1979) *Schooling the Smash Street Kids*. London: Macmillan.

Creighton, S.J. and Noyes, P. (1989) *Child Abuse Trends in England and Wales 1983–1987*. London: National Society for the Prevention of Cruelty to Children.

Crewe, I. (1974) Studying elites in Britain, in I. Crewe (ed.) *British Political Sociology Yearbook I: Elites in Western Democracy*. London: Croom Helm.

Critcher, C. (1996) On the waterfront: applying the flashpoints model to protest against live animal exports, in C. Critcher and D. Waddington (eds) *Policing Public Order: Theoretical and Practical Issues*. Aldershot: Avebury.

Daly, K. (1994) *Gender, Crime and Punishment*. New Haven, CT: Yale University Press.

Daly, K. (1998) Gender, crime and criminology, in M. Tonry (ed.) *The Handbook of Crime and Punishment*. Oxford: Oxford University Press.

Daly, K. and Chesney Lind, M. (1988) Feminism and criminology, *Justice Quarterly*, 5(4): 498–538.

Davies, A. (1999) These viragoes are no less cruel than the lads, *British Journal of Criminology*, 39(1): 72–89.

Davies, N. (1993) *Murder on Ward Four*. London: Chatto and Windus.

Dix, D. (1845) *Remarks on Prisons and Prison Discipline in the United States*, 2nd edn. Reprint 1967. Montclair, NJ: Patterson Smith.

Doan, L. (1997) 'Gross indecency between women': policing lesbians or policing lesbian police?, *Social and Legal Studies*, 6(4).

Dobash, R.E. and Dobash, R.P. (1987) The response of the British and American women's movements to violence against women, in J. Hanmer and M. Maynard (eds) *Women, Violence and Social Control*. London: Macmillan.

Dobash, R.E. and Dobash, R.P. (1992) *Women, Violence and Social Change*. London: Routledge.

Downes, D. and Morgan, R. (1997) Dumping the 'Hostages to Fortune'? The politics of law and order in post-war Britain, in M. Maguire, R. Morgan and R. Reiner (eds) *The Oxford Book of Criminology*, 2nd edn. Oxford: Clarendon Press.

Downes, D.M. and Rock, P.E. (1988) *Understanding Deviance*, 2nd edn. Oxford: Oxford University Press.

Durova, N. (1989) *The Cavalry Maiden*, translated by M.F. Zirin. Bloomington, IN: Indiana University Press.

Eaton, M.E. (2000) Frances Heidensohn: a woman in her own time, *Women and Criminal Justice*.

Edwards, S. (1989) *Policing 'Domestic' Violence*. London: Sage.

Enloe, C. (1988) *Does Khaki Become You?* London: Pandora.

Enloe, C. (1993) *The Morning After*. Berkeley, CA: University of California Press.

Ericson, R.V. and Haggerty, K.D. (1997) *Policing the Risk Society*. Oxford: Clarendon Press.

European Network of Policewomen (ENP) (1999) *European Network of Policewomen Annual Report.* ENP: Amersfoort.

Fairchild, E. (1987) Women police in Weimar: professionalism, politics and innovation in police organizations, *Law and Society Review*, 21(3): 375–402.

Faludi, S. (1991) *Backlash.* London: Chatto and Windus.

Faludi, S. (1999) *Stiffed.* London: Chatto and Windus.

Feeley, M. and Little, D. (1991) The vanishing female: the decline of women in the criminal process, 1687–1912, *Law and Society Review*, 25(4): 719–57.

Feinman, C. (1994) *Women in the Criminal Justice System*, 4th edn. New York, NY: Praeger.

Foucault, M. (1977) *Discipline and Punish.* New York, NY: Random House.

Garber, M. (1992) *Vested Interests.* Harmondsworth: Penguin.

Garland, D. (1985) *Punishment and Welfare.* Aldershot: Gower.

Garland, D. (1988) British criminology before 1935, in P. Rock (ed.) *A History of British Criminology.* Oxford: Oxford University Press.

Garland, D. (1992) Criminological knowledge and its relation to power: Foucault's genealogy, *British Journal of Criminology*, 32(4): 403–22.

Garland, D. (1994) Of crimes and criminals: the development of criminology in Britain, in M. Maguire, R. Morgan and R. Reiner (eds) *The Oxford Handbook of Criminology.* Oxford: Clarendon Press.

Gelsthorpe, L. (1997) Feminism and criminology, in M. Maguire, R. Morgan and R. Reiner (eds) *The Oxford Handbook of Criminology*, 2nd edn. Oxford: Clarendon Press.

Gelsthorpe, L. and Morris, A. (1988) Feminism and criminology in Britain, *British Journal of Criminology*, 28(2): 93–110.

Gelsthorpe, L. and Morris, A. (eds) (1990) *Feminist Perspectives in Criminology.* Buckingham: Open University Press.

Giddens, A. (1995) Living in a post-traditional society, in U. Beck, A. Giddens and S. Lash, *Reflexive Modernization.* Cambridge: Polity.

Giddens, A. (1999) *The Reith Lectures.* London: BBC Publications.

Goring, C. (1913) *The English Convict: A Statistical Study.* London: HMSO.

Gregory, J. and Lees, S. (1999) *Policing Sexual Assault.* London: Routledge.

Hanmer, J., Griffiths, S. and Jerwood, D. (1999) *Arresting Evidence: Domestic Violence and Repeat Victimisation*, Police research series paper 104. London: Home Office.

Hansson, D. (1995) Agenda-ing gender: feminism and engendering of academic criminology in South Africa, in N. Rafter and F.M. Heidensohn (eds) *International Feminist Perspectives in Criminology: Engendering a Discipline.* Buckingham: Open University Press.

Harrison, B. (1974) State intervention and moral reform in nineteenth century England, in P. Hollis (ed.) *Pressure from Without in Early Victorian England.* London: Edward Arnold.

Heidensohn, F.M. (1968) The deviance of women: a critique and an enquiry, *British Journal of Sociology*, 19(2): 160–75.

Heidensohn, F.M. (1985) *Women and Crime*. London: Macmillan and New York, NY: New York University Press.

Heidensohn, F.M. (1987) Questions for criminology, in P. Carlen and A. Worrall (eds) *Gender, Crime and Justice*. Milton Keynes: Open University Press.

Heidensohn, F.M. (1989) *Women in Policing in the USA*. London: Police Foundation.

Heidensohn, F.M. (1991) Women and crime in Europe, in F. Heidensohn and M. Farrell (eds) *Crime in Europe*. London: Routledge.

Heidensohn, F.M. (1992) *Women in Control? The Role of Women in Law Enforcement*. Oxford: Oxford University Press.

Heidensohn, F.M. (1994a) From being to knowing: some issues in the study of gender in contemporary society, *Women and Criminal Justice*, 6(1): 13–37.

Heidensohn, F.M. (1994b) We can handle it out here: women officers in Britain and the USA and the policing of public order, *Policing and Society*, 4(4): 293–303.

Heidensohn, F.M. (1995) Feminist perspectives and their impact on criminology and criminal justice in Britain, in N. Rafter and F.M. Heidensohn (eds) *International Feminist Perspectives in Criminology: Engendering a Discipline*. Buckingham: Open University Press.

Heidensohn, F.M. (1996a) Crime and policing, in V. Symes, C. Levy and J. Littlewood (eds) *The Future of Europe*. London: Macmillan.

Heidensohn, F.M. (1996b) *Taking Charge: Crime and Social Control in the Twenty-First Century*. London: Goldsmiths College, University of London.

Heidensohn, F.M. (1997a) Discovering sociology: further enquiries, in C. Ballard, J. Gubbay and C. Middleton (eds) *The Student's Companion to Sociology*. Oxford: Blackwell.

Heidensohn, F.M. (1997b) Sisters and strangers. Paper presented to American Society of Criminology Meetings, San Diego, CA, November.

Heidensohn, F.M. (1997c) Gender and crime, in M. Maguire, R. Morgan and R. Reiner (eds) *Oxford Handbook of Criminology*. Oxford: Oxford University Press.

Heidensohn, F.M. (1998a) ENP and its antecedents or how to succeed in European policing, *European Network of Policewomen Newsletter*, 8–9 March.

Heidensohn, F.M. (1998b) Comparative models of policing and the role of women officers, *International Journal of Police Science and Management*, 1(3): 215–26.

Heidensohn, F.M. (1998c) Criminal justice: security, social control and the hidden agenda, in H. Jones and S. MacGregor (eds) *Social Issues and Party Politics*. London: Routledge.

Heidensohn, F.M. with Silvestri, M. (1996) *Women and Crime*, 2nd edn. London: Macmillan.

Heimer, K. and De Coster, S. (1999) The gendering of violent delinquency, *Criminology*, 37(2): 277–317.

Hey, V. (1985) Getting away with murder: PMT and the press, in S. Laws, V. Hey and A. Eagan, *Seeing Red*. London: Hutchinson.

Hirschmann, N.J. (1997) The theory and practice of freedom: the case of battered women, in M.L. Shanley and U. Narayan (eds) *Reconstructing Political Theory*. Cambridge: Polity.

Hobbs, D. (1995) *Bad Business*. Oxford: Oxford University Press.

Holdaway, S. and Rock, P. (1998) Thinking about criminology: a reflection on theory within criminology, in S. Holdaway and P. Rock (eds) *Thinking about Criminology*. London: UCL Press.

Hollis, P. (1987) *Ladies Elect: Women in English Local Government, 1865–1914*. Oxford: Clarendon Press.

Home Office (1990) *Criminal Statistics 1989*. London: HMSO.

Home Office (1991) Detailed breakdown of figures on violent offences supplied by the Home Office statistical branch (supplied to the author on request).

Home Office (1999a) *Statistics on Women and the Criminal Justice System*. London: Home Office Research, Development and Statistics Directorate.

Home Office (1999b) *Reducing Crime and Tackling its Causes*. London: Home Office Communication Directorate.

Hough, M., Stanko, E. and Young, J. (1995) Whither, whether, wither criminology? Symposium, British Society of Criminology, London, June.

Hubbard, L. (1893) *The Englishwoman's Yearbook*.

Hunt, J. (1984) The development of rapport through the negotiation of gender in field work among police, *Human Organization*, 43(4): 283–95.

Innes, M. (1999) The media as an investigative resource in murder enquiries, *British Journal of Criminology*, 39(2): 268–86.

Jefferson, T. (1996) Introduction to 'Masculinities, Social Relations and Crime', *British Journal of Criminology*, 36(3): 337–47.

Jeffreys, S. (1985) *The Spinster and her Enemies: Feminism and Sexuality 1880–1930*. London: Pandora.

Jones, H. (1998) The road to 1997, in H. Jones and S. MacGregor (eds) *Social Issues and Party Politics*. London: Routledge.

Jones, S. (1986) *Policewomen and Equality*. London: Macmillan.

Jones, T., Newburn, T. and Smith, D. (1994) *Democracy and Policing*. London: Policy Studies Institute.

Joutsen, M. (ed.) (1999) *Five Issues in European Criminal Justice*. Helsinki: European Institute for Crime Prevention and Control (HEUNI).

Jupp, V. (1989) *Methods of Criminological Research*. London: Unwin Hyman.

Kirsta, A. (1994) *Deadlier than the Male*. London: HarperCollins.

Klein, D. (1995) Crime through gender's prism – feminist criminology in the United States, in N. Rafter and F.M. Heidensohn (eds) *International Feminist Perspectives in Criminology: Engendering a Discipline*. Buckingham: Open University Press.

Lake, M. (1998) The irrevocable woman: feminist conceptions of citizenship in Australia, 1900–1945, in J.B. Landes (ed.) *Feminism, the Public and the Private*. Oxford: Oxford University Press.

Lash, S. (1995) Refexivity and its doubles: structure, aesthetics, community, in V. Beck, A. Giddens and S. Lash, *Reflexive Modernization*. Cambridge: Polity.

Levi, M. (1994a) Violent crime, in M. Maguire, R. Morgan and R. Reiner (eds) *The Oxford Handbook of Criminology*. Oxford: Clarendon Press.

Levi, M. (1994b) *British Society of Criminology Newsletter*.

Levi, M. (1995) Correspondence, *British Journal of Criminology*, 35(1) 138–42.

Levine, P. (1994) 'Walking the streets in a way no decent woman should': women police in World War I, *Journal of Modern History*, March: 34–78.

Lewis, J. (1980) *The Politics of Motherhood: Child and Maternal Welfare in England 1900–1939*. London: Croom Helm.

Lewis, J. (1991) *Women and Social Action in Victorian and Edwardian England*. Aldershot: Edward Elgar.

Lloyd, A. (1995) *Doubly Deviant, Doubly Damned*. Harmondsworth: Penguin.

Lock, J. (1979) *The British Policewoman: Her Story*. London: Hale.

Lodge, D. (1983) *Small World*. Harmondsworth: Penguin.

Lovenduski, J. (1995) An emerging advocate: the equal opportunities commission in Great Britain, in D.M. Stetson and A.G. Mazur (eds) *Comparative State Feminism*. London: Sage.

Lovenduski, J. and Randall, V. (1993) *Contemporary Feminist Politics: Women and Power in Britain*. Oxford: Oxford University Press.

Lupton, C. (1994) The British Refuge Movement: the survival of an ideal, in C. Lupton and T. Gillespie (eds) *Working with Violence*. London: Macmillan.

Lupton, C. and Gillespie, T. (eds) (1994) *Working with Violence*. London: Macmillan.

McAdam, D. (1996) Conceptual origins, current problems, future directions, in D. McAdam (ed.) *Comparative Perspectives on Social Movements*. Cambridge: Cambridge University Press.

MacDonald, E. (1991) *Shoot the Women First*. London: Fourth Estate.

McHugh, P. (1980) *Prostitution and Victorian Social Reform*. New York, NY: St Martin's Press.

Macpherson, W.M. Sir (1999) *The Stephen Lawrence Inquiry*, Report of an Inquiry by Sir W.M. Macpherson of Cluny, CM4262–1. London: The Stationery Office.

Maher, L. (1997) *Sexed Work: Gender, Race and Resistance in a Brooklyn Drug Market.* Oxford: Clarendon Press.

Mahood, L. (1990) The Magdalene's friend, *Women's Studies International Forum,* 13(1/2): 49–61.

Mannheim, H. (ed.) (1960) *Pioneers in Criminology.* London: Stevens.

Martin, S. (1981) *Breaking and Entering.* Berkeley, CA: University of California Press.

Mazur, A.G. and Stetson, D.M. (1995) The case for state feminism, in D.M. Stetson and A.G. Mazur (eds) *Comparative State Feminism.* London: Sage.

Miller, J. (1998) Up it up: gender and the accomplishment of street robbery, *Criminology,* 36(1): 37–65.

Mooney, G. (1998) 'Remoralizing' the poor? Gender, class and philanthropy in Victorian Britain, in G. Lewis (ed.) *Forming Nation, Framing Welfare.* London: Routledge.

Morgan, R., Maguire, M. and Reiner, R. (1994) Introduction, in M. Maguire, R. Morgan and R. Reiner (eds) *The Oxford Handbook of Criminology.* Oxford: Clarendon Press.

Morrell, C. (1996) Octavia Hill and women's networks in housing, in A. Digby and J. Stewart (eds) *Gender, Health and Welfare.* London: Routledge.

Morrison, W. (1994) Criminology, modernity and the 'Truth' of the human condition: reflections on the melancholy of postmodernism, in D. Nelken (ed.) *The Futures of Criminology.* London: Sage.

Naffine, N. (1987) *Female Crime.* Sydney: Allen and Unwin.

National Criminal Justice Reference Seminar (NCJRS) (1998) *Women in Criminal Justice: A Twenty Year Update.* National Criminal Justice Reference Seminar, National Institute of Justice, Maryland.

National Society for the Prevention of Cruelty to Children (NSPCC) (S. Creighton) (1990) *Child Abuse in 1989,* research briefing no. 11. London: NSPCC.

Nelken, D. (ed.) (1994) *The Futures of Criminology.* London: Sage.

Nettl, P. (1969) *Rosa Luxemburg.* Oxford: Oxford University Press.

Newburn, T. (1999) *Understanding and Preventing Police Corruption: Lessons from the Literature.* London: Home Office.

Newburn, T. and Stanko, E.A. (eds) (1994) *Just Boys Doing Business.* London: Routledge.

Nienhaus, U. (1992) Einsatz für die 'Sittlichkeit': Die Anfänge der Weiblichen Polizei im Wilhelminischen Kaiserreich und in der Weimarer Republik, in A. Lüdtke (ed.) *'Sicherheit' und 'Wohlfahrt' Polizei, Gesellschaft und Herrschaft im 19 und 20 Jahrhundert.* Frankfurt am Main: Suhrkamp.

Oakley, A. (1998) Gender, methodology and people's ways of knowing: some problems with feminism and the paradigm debate in social science. *Sociology,* 32(4): 707–31.

Office for Victims of Crime (1998) *Initiatives to Combat Violence Against Women.* Washington, DC: Office of Justice Programmes.

Peto, D.O.G. (1992) *The Memoirs of Miss Dorothy Olivia Georgiana Peto.* Organising Committee for the European Conference on Equal Opportunities in Police, Bramshill.

Petrie, G. (1971) *A Singular Iniquity.* London: Macmillan.

Pitch, T. (1995) Feminist politics, crime, law and order in Italy, in N. Rafter and F.M. Heidensohn (eds) *International Feminist Perspectives in Criminology: Engendering a Discipline.* Buckingham: Open University Press.

Platek, M. (1995) What it's like for women: criminology in Poland and Eastern Europe, in N. Rafter and F.M. Heidensohn (eds) *International Feminist Perspectives in Criminology: Engendering a Discipline.* Buckingham: Open University Press.

Poe-Yamagata, E. (1996) *A Statistical Overview of Females in the Juvenile Justice System.* Pittsburgh, PA: Natt Centre for Juvenile Justice.

Polk, K. (1993) Homicide: women as offenders, in P. Easteal and S. McKillop (eds) *Women and the Law.* Canberra: Australian Institute of Criminology.

Pollak, O. (1950) *The Criminality of Women.* Philadelphia, PA: University of Pennsylvania Press.

Porter, S. (1996) Contra-Foucault: soldiers, nurses and power, *Sociology,* 30(1): 59–78.

Prenzler, T. (1994) Women in Australian policing: an historical overview, *Journal of Australian Studies,* 42 (September): 78–88.

Prenzler, T. (1998) Concession and containment: the establishment of women in the Queensland Police, 1931–1965, *Australian and New Zealand Journal of Criminology,* 31(2): 1–16.

Price, B.R. and Sokoloff, N.J. (eds) (1995) *The Criminal Justice System and Women Offenders, Victims and Workers,* 2nd edn. New York, NY: McGraw-Hill.

Prochaska, F. (1980) *Women and Philanthropy in Nineteenth Century England.* Oxford: Oxford University Press.

Pugh, M. (1992) *Women and the Women's Movement in Britain 1914–1959.* London: Macmillan.

Punch, M. (1989) Researching police deviance, *British Journal of Sociology,* 40: 177–204.

Radzinowicz, L. (1999) *Adventures in Criminology.* London: Routledge.

Rafter, N.H. (1992) *Partial Justice Women, Prisons, and Social Control.* New Brunswick, NJ: Transaction.

Rafter, N. and Heidensohn, F.M. (eds) (1995a) *International Feminist Perspectives in Criminology: Engendering a Discipline.* Buckingham: Open University Press.

Rafter, N. and Heidensohn, F. (1995b) Introduction: the development of feminist perspectives on crime, in N. Rafter and F. Heidensohn (eds)

International Perspectives in Criminology: Engendering a Discipline. Buckingham: Open University Press.

Randall, V. (1982) *Women and Politics*, 1st edn. London: Macmillan.

Randall, V. (1987) *Women and Politics*, 2nd edn. London: Macmillan.

Randall, V. (1996) Feminism and child daycare, *Journal of Social Policy*, 254: 485–527.

Randall, V. (1998) Gender and power: women engage the state, in V. Randall and G. Waylen (eds) *Gender, Politics and the State*. London: Routledge.

Randall, V. and Waylen, G. (eds) (1998) *Gender, Politics and the State*. London: Routledge.

Reiner, R. (1991) *Chief Constables*. Oxford: Oxford University Press.

Reiner, R. (1992) *The Politics of the Police*, 2nd edn. Brighton: Harvester Wheatsheaf.

Reinharz, S. (1984) *On Becoming a Social Scientist*. New Brunswick, NJ: Transaction.

Rendall, J. (1985) *The Origins of Modern Feminism*. London: Macmillan.

Reynolds, A. (1991) *Tightrope*. London: Sidgwick and Jackson.

Rock, P.E. (1973) *Deviant Behaviour*. London: Hutchinson.

Rock, P.E. (1979) *The Making of Symbolic Interactionism*. London: Macmillan.

Rock, P.E. (1987) *A View from the Shadows: The Ministry of the Solicitor General of Canada and the Justice for Victims of Crime Initiative*. Oxford: Clarendon Press.

Rock, P.E. (1988a) The present state of criminology in Britain, *British Journal of Criminology*, 28(2): 188–99.

Rock, P.E. (1988b) Governments, victims and policies in two countries, *British Journal of Criminology*, 28(1): 44–66.

Rock, P.E. (1993) *The Social World of an English Crown Court*. Oxford: Clarendon Press.

Rock, P.E. (1994) The social organization of British criminology, in M. Maguire, R. Morgan and R. Reiner (eds) *The Oxford Handbook of Criminology*. Oxford: Clarendon Press.

Rock, P.E. (1996) *Reconstructing a Women's Prison: The Holloway Redevelopment Project 1968–1988*. Oxford: Clarendon Press.

Rock, P. and Holdaway, S. (1998) Thinking about criminology: 'facts are bits of biography', in S. Holdaway and P. Rock (eds) *Thinking about Criminology*. London: UCL Press.

Roshier, B. (1989) *Controlling Crime: The Classical Perspective in Criminology*. Milton Keynes: Open University Press.

Rowbotham, S. (1992) *Women in Movement*. London: Routledge.

Rupp, L. (1994) Constructing internationalism: the case of transnational women's organization 1888–1945, *American Historical Review*, 99: 1571–600.

Ryan, M.P. (1983) The power of women's networks, in J. Newton, M.P. Ryan and J. Walkowitz (eds) *Sex and Class in Women's History*. London: Routledge and Kegan Paul.

Ryan, M.P. (1998) Gender and public access: women's politics in nineteenth century America, in J.B. Landes (ed.) *Feminism, the Public and the Private*. Oxford: Oxford University Press.

Sawer, M. (1995) 'Femocrats in glass towers?': the office of the status of women in Australia, in D.M. Stetson and A.G. Mazur (eds) *Comparative State Feminism*. London: Sage.

Schulz, D.M. (1995) *From Social Worker to Crime Fighter: Women in US Municipal Policing*. Westport, CT: Praeger.

Schulz, D. (1998) Bridging boundaries: United States policewomen's efforts to form an international network, *International Journal of Police Science and Management*, 1(1): 70–81.

Shacklady Smith, L. (1978) Sexist assumptions and female delinquency, in C. Smart and B. Smart (eds) *Women Sexuality and Social Control*. London: Routledge and Kegan Paul.

Shaw, M. (1998) Conflicting agendas: evaluating feminist programmes for women offenders. Unpublished PhD thesis, University of Nottingham.

Sheptycki, J.W.E. (1995) Transnational policing and the makings of the post-modern state, *British Journal of Criminology*, 35(4): 613–35.

Sheptycki, J.W.E. (1998) Policing, post-modernism and transnationalization, *British Journal of Criminology*, 38(3): 485–503.

Sherman, L., Gottfredson, D., Mackenzie, D., Eck, J., Reuter, P. and Bushway, S. (1998) *Preventing Crime: What Works, What Doesn't, What's Promising*. Washington, DC: National Institute of Justice.

Silvestri, M. (forthcoming) Visions of the future: the role of women in senior management in the police. Unpublished PhD thesis, University of London.

Simpson, S. (1991) Caste, class and violent crime: explaining difference in female offending, *Criminology*, 29(1): 115–35.

Sklar, K., Schüler, A. and Strasser, S. (eds) (1998) *Social Justice Feminists in the US and Germany*. Ithaca, NY and London: Cornell University Press.

Smart, C. (1977) *Women, Crime and Criminology*. London: Routledge and Kegan Paul.

Smart, C. (1989) *Feminism and the Power of Law*. London: Routledge.

Smart, C. (1990) Feminist approaches to criminology or postmodern woman means atavistic man, in L. Gelsthorpe and A. Morris (eds) *Feminist Perspectives in Criminology*. Buckingham: Open University Press.

Smith, D.E. (1989) *The Everyday World as Problematic*. Milton Keynes: Open University Press.

Smith, D. and Gray, J. (1981) *Police and People of London*. London: Policy Studies Institute.

Smithies, E. (1982) *Crime in Wartime*. London: Allen and Unwin.

South, N. (1996) Late-modern criminology: 'late' as in 'dead' or 'modern' as in 'new'?, in D. Owen (ed.) *After Sociology? Contemporary Reflections on the State of the Discipline*. London: Sage.

Sparks, R. (1999) Review of Radzinowicz 1999, *British Journal of Criminology*, 39(3): 452–5.

Sperling, V. (1998) Gender, politics and the state during Russia's transition period, in V. Randall and G. Waylen (eds) *Gender, Politics and the State*. London: Routledge.

Stanko, E. (1990) *Everyday Violence*. London: Pandora.

Stanko, E.A. (1998) Gender and policy making. Paper presented to the National Institute of Social Work Seminar, London, May.

Stark, S. (1998) *Female Tars*. London: Pimlico.

Stetson, D.M. and Mazur, A.G. (eds) (1995) *Comparative State Feminism*. London: Sage.

Strachey, R. (1978) *The Cause*. London: Bell and Sons.

Summers, A. (1979) A home from home – women's philanthropic work in the CIG, in S. Burman (ed.) *Fit Work for Women*. London: Croom Helm.

Sumner, C. (1994) *The Sociology of Deviance: An Obituary*. Buckingham: Open University Press.

Tancred, E. (1931) Women police abroad, *Police Journal*, 4: 175–87.

Taylor, I., Walton, P. and Young, J. (1973) *The New Criminology*. London: Routledge and Kegan Paul.

Taylor, V. (1999) Gender and social movements, *Gender and Society*, 13(1): 8–33.

Taylor, V. and Whittier, N. (1995) Analytical approaches to social movement culture, in H. Johnston and B. Klaudemans (eds) *Social Movements and Culture*. Minneapolis, MN: University of Minnesota Press.

Thomas, E. (1967) *The Women Incendiaries*. London: Secker and Warburg.

Timmins, N. (1995) *The Five Giants: A Biography of the Welfare State*. London: Fontana.

Tomsen, S. (1997) A top night: social protest, masculinity and the culture of drinking violence, *British Journal of Criminology*, 37(1): 90–102.

Van Maanen, J. (1988) *Tales of the Field*. Chicago: University of Chicago Press.

Vicinus, M. (1985) *Independent Women: Work and Community for Single Women 1850–1920*. London: Virago.

Waddington, P.A.J. (1999) Police (canteen) sub-culture: an appreciation, *British Journal of Criminology*, 39(2): 286–309.

Walby, S. (1997) *Gender Transformations*. London: Routledge.

Walkowitz, J. (1980) *Prostitution and Victorian Society*. Cambridge: Cambridge University Press.

Waylen, G. (1998) Gender, feminism and the state: an overview, in V. Randall and G. Waylen (eds) *Gender, Politics and the State*. London: Routledge.

Wellford, C. (1997) Controlling crime and achieving justice, *Criminology*, 35(1): 1–11.

Wilczynski, A. (1997) Mad or bad? Child-killers, gender and the courts, *British Journal of Criminology*, 37(3): 419–36.

Willis, P. (1977) *Learning to Labour: How Working Class Kids Get Working Class Jobs*. London: Saxon House.

Wiltsher, A. (1985) *Most Dangerous Women*. London: Pandora.

Wolfgang, M.E., Figlio, R.M. and Thornberry, T.P. (eds) (1978) *Evaluating Criminology*. New York, NY: Elsevier.

Woodiwiss, A. (1996) Searching for signs of globalisation, *Sociology*, 30(4): 799–810.

Wright, R. (1995) The most-cited scholars in criminology: a comparison of textbooks and journals, *Journal of Criminal Justice*, 23: 303–11.

Wright, R. (1996) The most-cited scholars in criminology and criminal justice textbooks, 1989 to 1993, *The Justice Professional*.

Wright, R.A. and Sheridan, C. (1997) The most-cited scholars and works in women and crime publications, *Women and Criminal Justice*, 9(2): 41–60.

Wyles, L. (1951) *A Woman at Scotland Yard*. London: Faber.

Yeatman, A. (1990) *Bureaucrats, Technocrats, Femocrats*. Sydney: Allen and Unwin.

Young, J. (1988) Risk of crime and fear of crime: a realist critique of survey-based assumptions, in M. Maguire and J. Pointing (eds) *Victims of Crime*. Milton Keynes: Open University Press.

Young, J. (1994) Incessant chatter: recent paradigms in criminology, in M. Maguire, R. Morgan and R. Reiner (eds) *The Oxford Handbook of Criminology*. Oxford: Clarendon Press.

Young, J. (1999) *The Exclusive Society*. London: Sage.

Young, M. (1991) *An Inside Job*. Oxford: Clarendon Press.

Young, P. (1992) The importance of utopias in criminological thinking, *British Journal of Criminology*, 32(4): 423–37.

Zalm, M. (1999) Thoughts on the future of criminology, in *Criminology*, 37(1): 1–16.

Zedner, L. (1991) *Women, Crime and Custody in Victorian England*. Oxford: Oxford University Press.

Zedner, L. (1997) Victims, in M. Maguire, R. Morgan and R. Reiner (eds) *The Oxford Book of Criminology*, 2nd edn. Oxford: Clarendon Press.

Zimring, F.E. and Hawkins, G. (1997) *Crime is Not the Problem: Lethal Violence in America*. Oxford: Oxford University Press.

index

UNDERSTANDING CRIMINOLOGY
CURRENT THEORETICAL DEBATES

Sandra Walklate

This clear and approachable text provides a critical overview of the criminological enterprise over the past twenty years. The author is concerned to identify the continuities underpinning criminological theory and to situate these continuities within a contemporary criminological and political context. She offers the student an in-depth appreciation of criminological theorizing paying particular attention to left realism, right realism and the influence of feminism. A detailed exploration is also undertaken of the interface between the substantive concerns of criminological and social policy. Drawing particularly on a critical understanding of current political concerns about crime, Walklate sets out a framework for the future development of criminological work informed by the notions of social justice, risk and trust.

Sandra Walklate's *Understanding Criminology* is a well structured theoretical text for undergraduates in criminology and criminal justice, including clear summaries and suggestions for further reading. It will also have considerable appeal to students of sociology with an interest in crime and justice, as well as professionals in criminal justice, probation and social work.

Contents

168pp   0 335 19361 7 (Paperback)   0 335 19362 5 (Hardback)

INTERNATIONAL FEMINIST PERSPECTIVES IN CRIMINOLOGY
ENGENDERING A DISCIPLINE

Nicole Hahn Rafter and Frances Heidensohn

- What impact has feminism had on criminology in various countries around the world?
- Are developments unique in each setting or are there key generalizations to be made?

This is the first book which brings together an international range of contributors who outline and analyse the impact of feminism on criminology in their countries. Feminist perspectives have challenged the very basis of conventional criminology and have profoundly altered the understanding of crimes such as domestic violence and the abuse of children. This book is essential reading for all those interested in new approaches to crime and criminology. It provides a splendid overview, and enables international comparisons to be made, thus encouraging globalization of this field. This is the first multicultural book in the field of criminology.

Contents
Introduction – The South – Feminist criminology in Australia – Europe – Feminist perspectives and their impact on criminology and criminal justice in Britain – Feminist politics, crime, law and order in Italy – The place and status of feminist criminology in Germany, Denmark, Norway and Finland – What it's like for women: criminology in Poland and Eastern Europe – North America – Canadian criminology and the woman question – From patriarchy to gender: feminist theory, criminology and the challenge of diversity – The 'dark figure' of criminology: towards a black and multi-ethnic feminist agenda for theory and research – Crime through gender's prism: feminist criminology in the United States – Index.

272pp   0 335 19389 7 (Paperback)   0 335 19388 9 (Hardback)

ENGENDERING SOCIAL POLICY

Sophie Watson and Lesley Doyal

Engendering Social Policy brings new and fresh perspectives to the
question of how social policy constructs gendered social relations.
With the restructuring of welfare firmly back on the political
agenda, in the context of a reassertion that traditional families are
the backbone of society, this book raises important issues for students, academics and practitioners grappling with social policy
issues at the end of the millennium.

Articles in the collection draw on a diversity of theoretical and
methodological perspectives engaging with issues that have vexed
feminist analysts and activists over more than two decades. The
collection explores how social policy constructs gendered relations,
the difference/equality debate, representations and discourses of
gender in social policy, the tensions and issues associated with
restructuring domestic relations, and feminist alternatives to mainstream social policy solutions. The book adopts a comparative and
international perspective taking on board the importance of global
changes as well as illustrating its argument with practices and
research from a number of countries.

This book is essential reading for those interested in seriously
addressing questions of gender and social policy in an international
framework.

Contents

224pp   0 335 20113 X (Paperback)   0 335 20114 8 (Hardback)